MW01155051

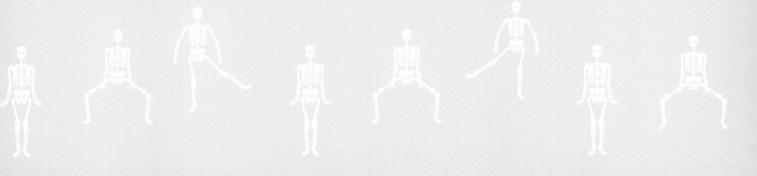

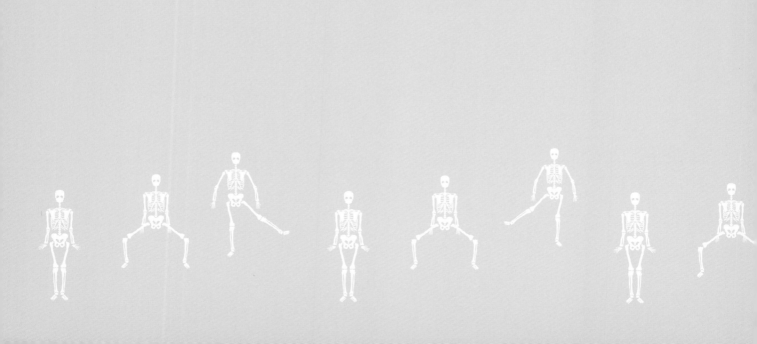

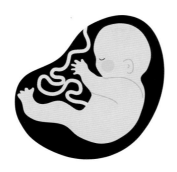

THE HUMAN BODY AT A GLANCE

Text by
Cristina Peraboni

Illustrations by
Giulia De Amicis

WHITE STAR KIDS

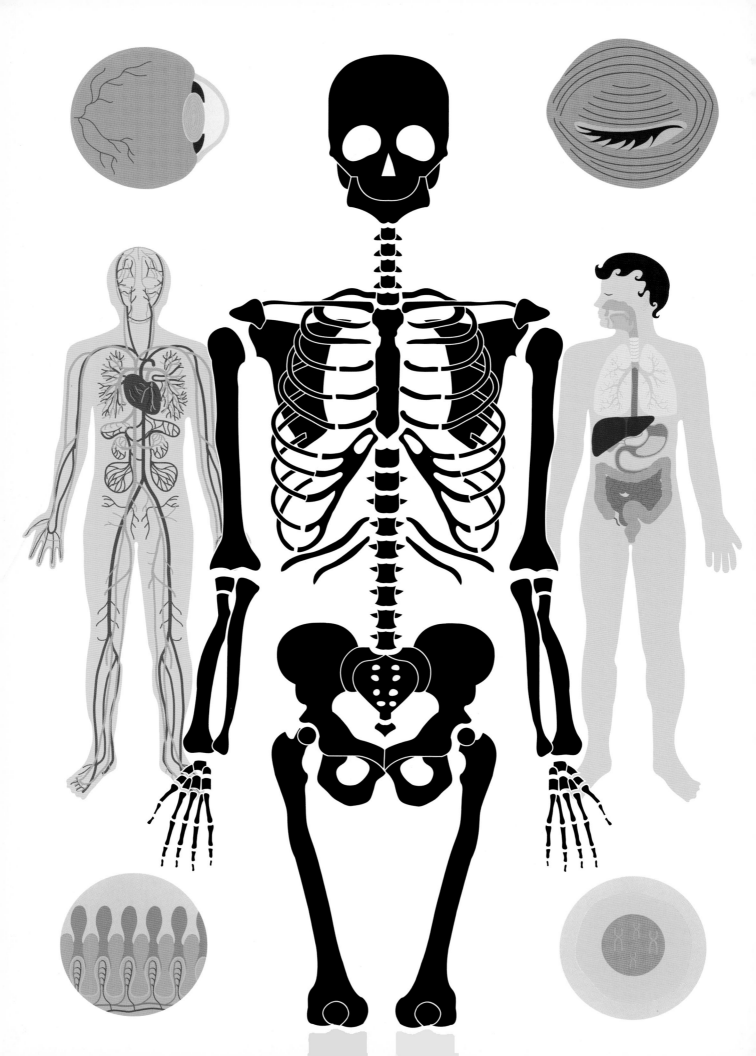

INDEX

Introduction

IF YOU ARE THE NOSY TYPE, THEN THIS IS THE RIGHT BOOK FOR YOU.
This isn't just a book about the human body, its parts, and how it works. You will discover **your body** in a slightly different way. Along with **figures** and **measurements**, you will find out about the most bizarre characteristics of your body and, most importantly... YOU WILL COMPARE THEM WITH THOSE OF ANIMALS!

What will you find in this book?

Many, many facts explained with easy and exciting illustrations.

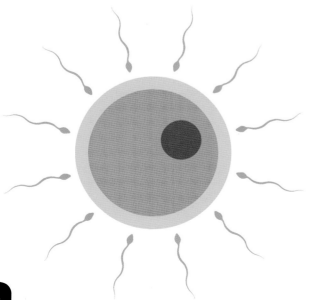

Just imagine your body as a complex **construction toy** game: HOW MANY BRICKS IS IT MADE UP OF? AND HOW ARE THEY STRUCTURED TO MAKE THE BODY FUNCTION?
The bricks are the **cells**; you will learn about their extraordinary complexity and variety and you will find out that, in the world of living creatures, NOT ALL CELLS ARE AS SMALL AS YOU MIGHT IMAGINE THEM TO BE.

The human body, like the body of every other animal, works like a **machine**. It needs a computer that controls the correct functioning of all the components: the **brain**. The human brain is, however, much more complicated than a normal computer. After all, it was our brain that created the computer...

... while a computer may never be able to create and build a human brain!

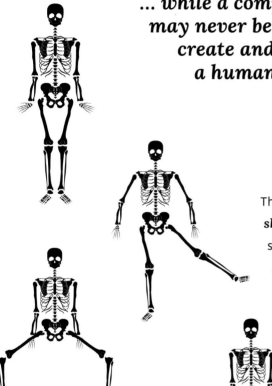

The frame that supports our body is the **skeleton**, however it is not fixed like the scaffolding that we put up to build a house. Many of the pieces of the skeleton can move thanks to particular connections called **joints**.

Other pieces are strongly fixed together to provide robust protection, such as the pieces forming the **skull**, which enclose the brain.

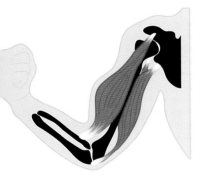

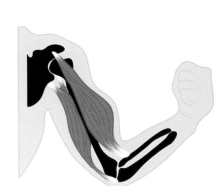

A complex motor system is wrapped around the skeleton: the **muscles**. There are many different types of muscles because we need one muscle for each different movement: to lift or lower an arm, to open or close the mouth, etc. If you think about all the parts of your body that you can move, you can easily understand why we have so many muscles. SO HOW MANY MUSCLES ARE THERE? AND WHAT IS THEIR ANATOMY?

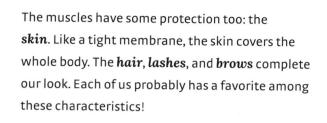

The muscles have some protection too: the *skin*. Like a tight membrane, the skin covers the whole body. The **hair**, **lashes**, and **brows** complete our look. Each of us probably has a favorite among these characteristics!

Animals feature coats and colorful plumages too, but they don't follow the latest trends like humans do!

In the center of the body is a very special ticking clock: the **heart**. It beats throughout our lives without stopping, with a precise rhythm that is different for each animal. The heart makes the **blood** flow and supplies each part of the body with the nutrients it needs.

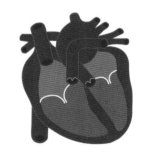

YOU DON'T HAVE TO CONTROL IT, IT WORKS BY ITSELF. When you run, it beats faster to give you more energy, and when you are calm and relaxed, it returns to its normal beat.

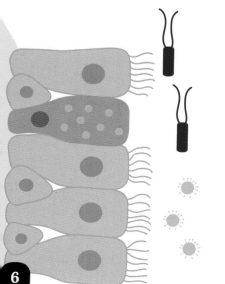

Your **breathing** is automatic too. You breathe throughout your whole life, night and day. The rhythm of your breathing can change automatically. After a run, it becomes much faster. We call this "panting."

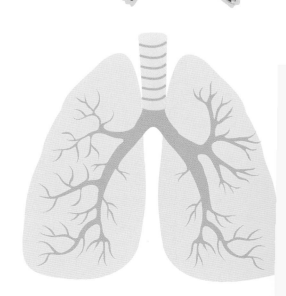

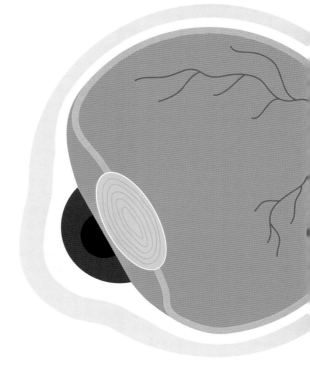

Finally, you have the senses, which help you live within the environment. Thanks to them, you can smell, taste, see, and hear.

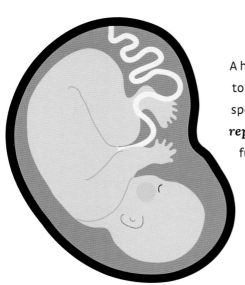

A human being doesn't just possess the tools to survive as an individual. Like all other species, humans also have the **ability to reproduce**, which ensures that there will be future generations. You will discover the secrets behind the development of a human being, from an embryo to a newborn baby.

When growing up, a child *will resemble its parents*, but it will not be completely identical to them. WHY? WHAT REGULATES THIS MECHANISM? COULD IT HAVE SOMETHING TO DO WITH THE FAMOUS DNA?

And now get ready to be surprised, as the following pages are packed with lots of funny and entertaining facts!

The cells

The bricks of life

Our body is made up of cells that work with one another to make the whole body function. A cell is like a small living creature: it feeds, breathes, and eliminates waste, just like you.

Tissues

The tissues of the human body are numerous and different from one another, but WE CAN GROUP THEM INTO FOUR MAIN TYPES:

How many cells are there in the human body?

A MULTIMILLION-DOLLAR QUESTION.
While we know exactly how many **bones** and how many **muscles** we have, it is a bit different when it comes to **cells**. Their quantity depends on numerous factors: a child will have fewer cells than an adult, but an adult can be slim and small and so might have fewer cells than another adult who is tall and robust.

IT IS IMPOSSIBLE TO CALCULATE THE NUMBER EXACTLY.
Someone tried, though. According to calculations, a 30-year-old male, 5.6 ft (1.70 m) tall and weighing 176.3 lb (80 kg) has roughly **37.2 TRILLION CELLS!**

Different cells form different tissues.

The word "**tissue**" makes you think of FABRICS and CLOTHES, however, when studying a human body under the microscope, this word refers to DIFFERENT GROUPS OF CELLS THAT CARRY OUT A SPECIFIC FUNCTION.

The heart, the bones, the skin, and all the other organs are made up of different **tissues**. Each tissue is made up of GROUPS OF SIMILAR CELLS that all have the same function.

Small and minuscule

Most cells are so small that they can only be seen through a MICROSCOPE.

That is why CELLS ARE MEASURED IN MICRONS. Each micron corresponds to one millionth of a meter. This means that, in order to form one meter, you need to line up one million microns!

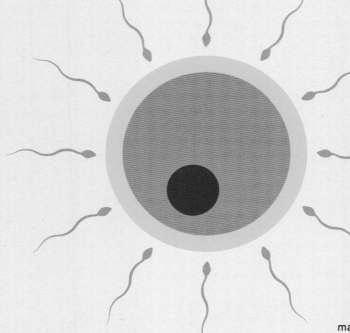

Egg
120 microns

Spermatozoon
5 microns

THE BIGGEST CELL IN THE BODY is in the female body. It's the **egg**, a round cell measuring up to **120 microns**, like a tiny grain of sand. It is the only cell VISIBLE TO THE NAKED EYE.

THE SMALLEST CELL IN THE BODY is in the male body, and it is the cell that tries to fuse with the biggest cell to create a new life. We are talking about the **spermatozoon**, which measures up to **5 microns**. It is very small, but its tail is **50 microns** long!

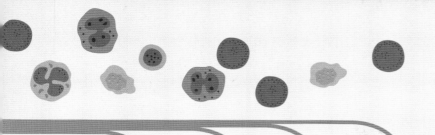

MUSCULAR

Muscular tissue makes up the **muscles** and wraps the **bones** and the **organs**. Its cells ARE ELONGATED and are called **fibers**.

1

CONNECTIVE

Connective tissue occupies spaces left empty by other tissues, linking them together. ITS CELLS ARE VERY DIFFERENT FROM ONE ANOTHER, depending on whether they are in the **bones**, in the **blood**, or in the **fat**.

2

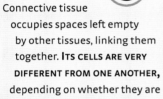

NERVOUS

Nervous tissue makes up the **brain**, the **spinal cord,** and the **nerves**. Its cells can have VERY DIFFERENT shapes and dimensions.

3

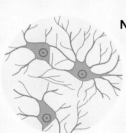

EPITHELIAL

Epithelial tissue wraps **the whole body** and produces **hair, teeth,** and **nails**. Its cells are TIGHTLY PACKED together.

4

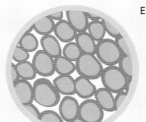

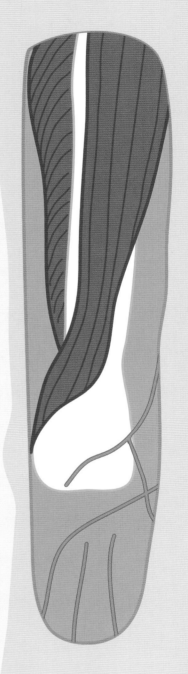

What about animals?

EGG COMPARISON:
In the animal world, the biggest cells are the *eggs*.

If we take a chicken egg as an example, we need to make a distinction. **THE REAL CELL IS ONLY THE YOLK.** The white and the shell are considered "*extracellular*."

HOWEVER, IT STILL IS AN ENORMOUS CELL...!

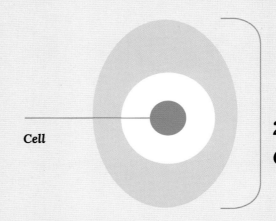

Cell

2.3 in (6 cm)
Chicken egg

To make up an ostrich egg, the biggest in the world, we need...

...24
chicken eggs.

7 in (18 cm)
Ostrich egg

The biggest ever

<small>**THAT'S NOT ALL:**</small>
In the past, we used to have an even bigger cell, the **egg of the elephant bird** (*Aepyornis*). The elephant bird used to live in Madagascar and became extinct a thousand years ago.

14 in (35 cm)
Elephant bird egg

To make up an elephant bird egg, we need...

...150
chicken eggs!

9.8 ft (300 cm)

9.2 ft (280 cm)

5.9 ft (180 cm)

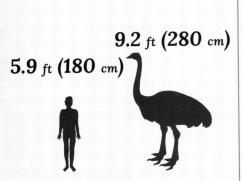

HUMAN   OSTRICH

ELEPHANT BIRD

The brain

The control panel

The brain is the most complex organ in the body. Scientists all over the world study its functions, but they are still far from understading it completely.

The brain controls:

HEART

LUNGS

MUSCLES

STOMACH

The **brain** is in charge of the entire system that controls the body: the **nervous system**.

FASTER THAN THE FASTEST OF COMPUTERS, the brain conducts **EVERYTHING THAT HAPPENS IN THE BODY** like an orchestra conductor. It tells the **muscles** when and how to move. It gives the input which allows the **heart** to beat and the **lungs** to breathe, and it alerts the stomach when it is time to eat. It makes us feel emotions and lets us laugh, cry, or get angry.

It allows you to absorb new information, just like you're doing now!

The cortex

Seen from above, the human brain looks like a WALNUT KERNEL, but the deep folds visible on its surface are more numerous than on the surface of a walnut. They are called **cerebral circumvolutions**.

It is exactly this "folded" part, the **cortex**, that makes us MORE INTELLIGENT THAN ANIMALS.

The cortex hosts the ABILITIES TYPICAL OF HUMANS: thought, memory, attention, conscience, and many others.

All the organs in the body are **innervated**, which means that they are equipped with many filaments. These filaments are similar to thin electrical cables.

The filaments are called **nerves**, and are the projections of the **axons**. Their function is to SEND SIGNALS TO THE BRAIN on the one hand and to FOLLOW ITS ORDERS on the other.

The brain has a consistency similar to that of pudding.

The neurons

The nervous cells inside the brain are called **neurons**. They receive impulses from the body and send impulses out to other organs.

The neuron is a cell with a very strange shape. WE CAN COMPARE IT TO A TREE because it has a trunk, called an **axon**, and many branches, known as **dendrites**.

Thanks to the dendrites and the axon, each neuron CAN CONNECT WITH THOUSANDS OF OTHER NEURONS, thus creating a very intricate web, along which run the **nerve impulses**.

dendrites

nucleus

axons

IT HAS BEEN CALCULATED THAT A HUMAN BRAIN CONTAINS ABOUT 86 BILLION NEURONS. Although this sounds like a huge number, once they are all grouped together, the neurons actually occupy only a small part of the brain. 75% OF THE BRAIN IS MADE UP OF WATER, and the **neurons** are immersed in a kind of **jelly**. This is why the brain's consistency reminds us of pudding!

THE HUMAN BRAIN WEIGHS ABOUT

3.1 lb (1.4 kg)

75%
water

What about animals?

Animals have cortexes which are much less developed than ours. Their brains look less "folded." A *mouse* and a *rabbit*, for example, have almost completely smooth brains.

The only animal that has a cortex with higher numbers of circumvolutions than ours is the *dolphin*. Dolphins are extremely intelligent creatures THAT CAN FEEL EMOTIONS SIMILAR TO OURS!

RABBIT

CAT

SHEEP

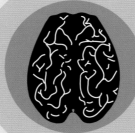

CHIMPANZEE

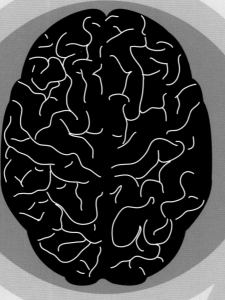

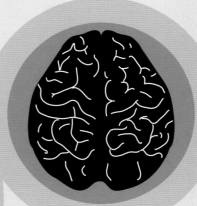

HUMAN

Despite making up only **2% OF OUR BODY WEIGHTS**, the human brain burns almost a quarter of the entire energy produced by the body. It is extremely sensitive to a lack of *oxygen*, because it uses it up more than any other organ.

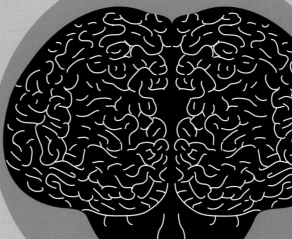

DOLPHIN

A bit of history

The evolution of the human brain

TODAY THE HUMAN BRAIN WEIGHS ABOUT 3.1 LB (1.4 KG). However, this is the result of a transformation that happened over **5 million years,** starting when the first **hominids** appeared on Earth.

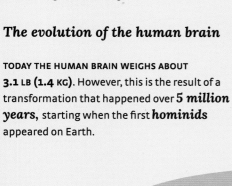
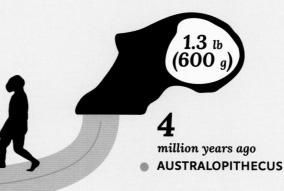

1.3 _lb_ **(600** _g_ **)**

4

million years ago
● **AUSTRALOPITHECUS**

Paleontologists, i.e. the scientists who study fossils, discovered that **Australopithecus** – the first primate to walk on two legs – had a brain as big as that of a **chimpanzee** and a FACE THAT PROTRUDED FORWARD VERY FAR.

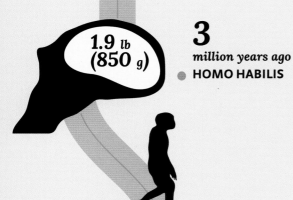

1.9 _lb_ **(850** _g_ **)**

3

million years ago
● **HOMO HABILIS**

During the course of millions of years, the face of the hominids' descendants became flatter and flatter, whereas their skulls became rounder and rounder.

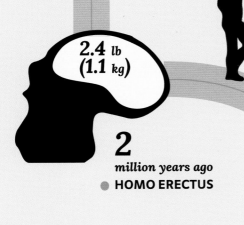

2.4 _lb_ **(1.1** _kg_ **)**

2

million years ago
● **HOMO ERECTUS**

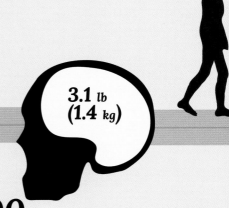

3.1 _lb_ **(1.4** _kg_ **)**

300

thousand years ago
● **HOMO SAPIENS**

The skeleton

A *natural scaffolding*

In vertebrate creatures, the skeleton is made up of bones.
Fish, amphibians, reptiles, birds, and all mammals have skeletons.
And within the skeleton, each bone has a precise position.

The functions of the skeleton

SUPPORT AND MOVEMENT
The **skeleton** is a structure without which the body would be a **SHAPELESS MASS**. The bones in the skeleton are connected to one another by **joints** such as the elbow, the knee. and the shoulder. **Bones, joints,** and **muscles** create a whole system of axes, levers, and pliers that ALLOW US TO PERFORM ALL OF OUR DAILY ACTIONS.

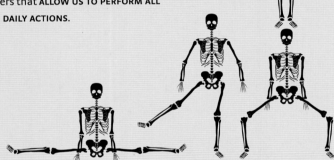

PROTECTION
Some parts of the skeleton are tasked with **protecting** particularly delicate organs. The **brain** is encased in the **skull**, and the **heart** and the **lungs** are protected inside the **ribcage**. The **vertebrae** surround and protect the **spinal cord**.

PRODUCTION OF BLOOD CELLS
Nature always tries to save on energy and space. Along with the fundamental function of supporting the body, it has assigned another task to the bones, which has nothing to do with movement. THE SUBSTANCE THAT PRODUCES BLOOD CELLS, THE **bone marrow**, IS ACTUALLY INSIDE THE BONES!

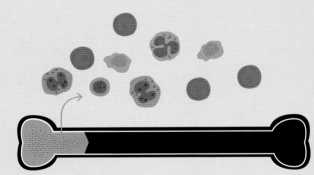

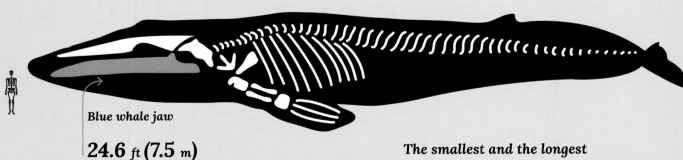

Blue whale jaw

24.6 ft (7.5 m)

Do you know what the biggest bone in the world is?
IT IS NOT A DINOSAUR'S BONE. It belongs instead to the BIGGEST ANIMAL EVER TO HAVE LIVED ON OUR PLANET: the **blue whale**. Its **jaw** can measure up to **24.6 ft (7.5 m)**!

The smallest and the longest

THE SMALLEST BONE is in the middle ear and is called the **stapes**: 0.16 in (4 mm).

smallest

THE LONGEST BONE in our skeleton is the **femur**. On average, it is 19 in (48 cm) long.

longest

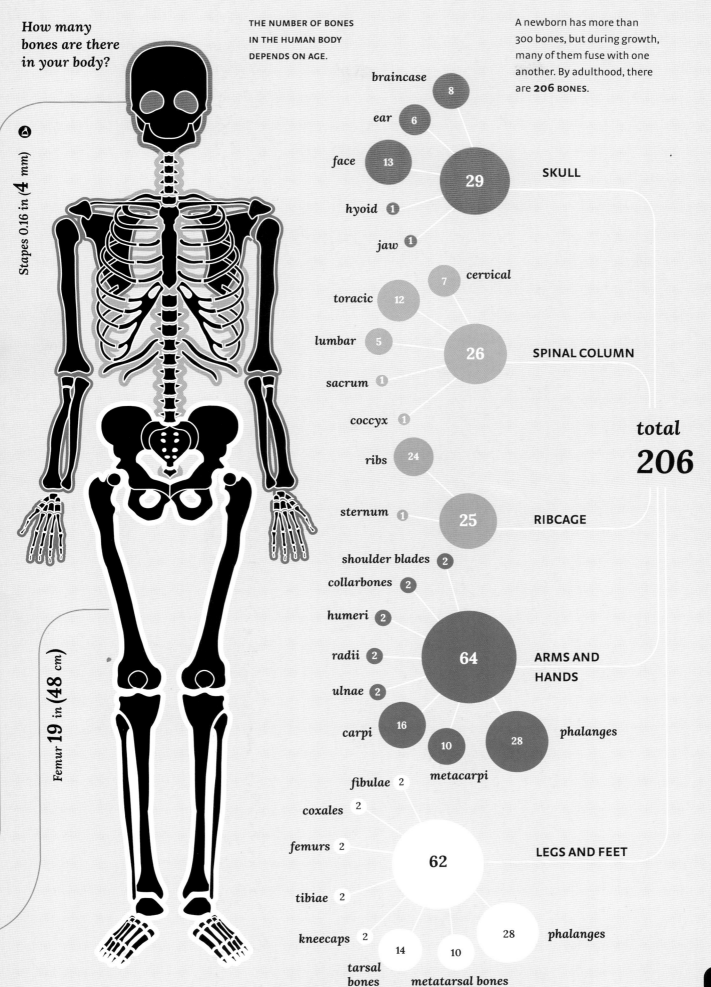

How many bones are there in your body?

THE NUMBER OF BONES IN THE HUMAN BODY DEPENDS ON AGE.

A newborn has more than 300 bones, but during growth, many of them fuse with one another. By adulthood, there are **206** BONES.

Stapes 0.16 in (**4** mm)

braincase 8
ear 6
face 13
hyoid 1
jaw 1

29 SKULL

cervical 7
toracic 12
lumbar 5
sacrum 1
coccyx 1

26 SPINAL COLUMN

ribs 24
sternum 1

25 RIBCAGE

total 206

shoulder blades 2
collarbones 2
humeri 2
radii 2
ulnae 2
carpi 16
metacarpi 10
phalanges 28

64 ARMS AND HANDS

Femur 19 in (**48** cm)

fibulae 2
coxales 2
femurs 2
tibiae 2
kneecaps 2
tarsal bones 14
metatarsal bones 10
phalanges 28

62 LEGS AND FEET

A bit of history

The human being is one of the few mammals that doesn't walk on four legs, i.e. is a biped.

Has it always been like this?

Our oldest ancestor, **Australopithecus**, WAS ALREADY A BIPED, even though his skull, and therefore his **brain**, WAS AS BIG AS THAT OF A CHIMPANZEE!

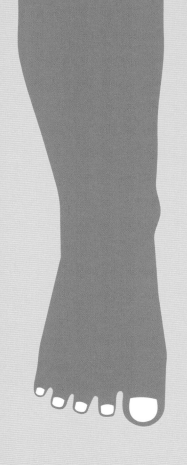

AVERAGE HEIGHT

4.6 ft
(140 cm**)**
(male)

3.4 ft
(105 cm**)**
(female)

While studying the **FIRST HOMINIDS FROM 4-5 MILLION YEARS AGO,** paleontologists discovered that **bipedalism** was **THE FIRST HUMAN CHARACTERISTIC TO APPEAR.**

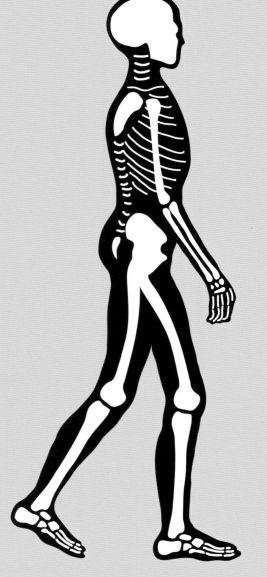

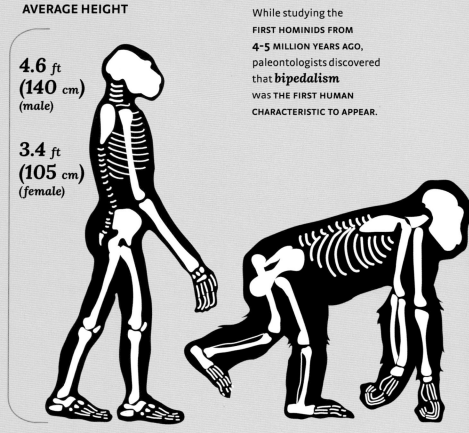

MODERN MAN

AUSTRALOPITHECUS

CHIMPANZEE

Arms comparison

CAN YOU RECOGNIZE YOUR ARM AND YOUR HAND AMONG THESE?
Of course you can, so try and guess who the rest of the arms here belong to.
Study the drawings. Bones of the same color are **homologous** (their appearances are similar).
In each of the featured animals, bones have transformed both in **shape** and **number** to adapt to a particular lifestyle. CAN YOU FIGURE OUT WHAT THEIR FUNCTIONS MIGHT BE?

YOU CAN FIND THE ANSWERS AT THE BOTTOM OF THE PAGE!

humerus

ulna

radius

carpal bones

metacarpal bones and phalanges

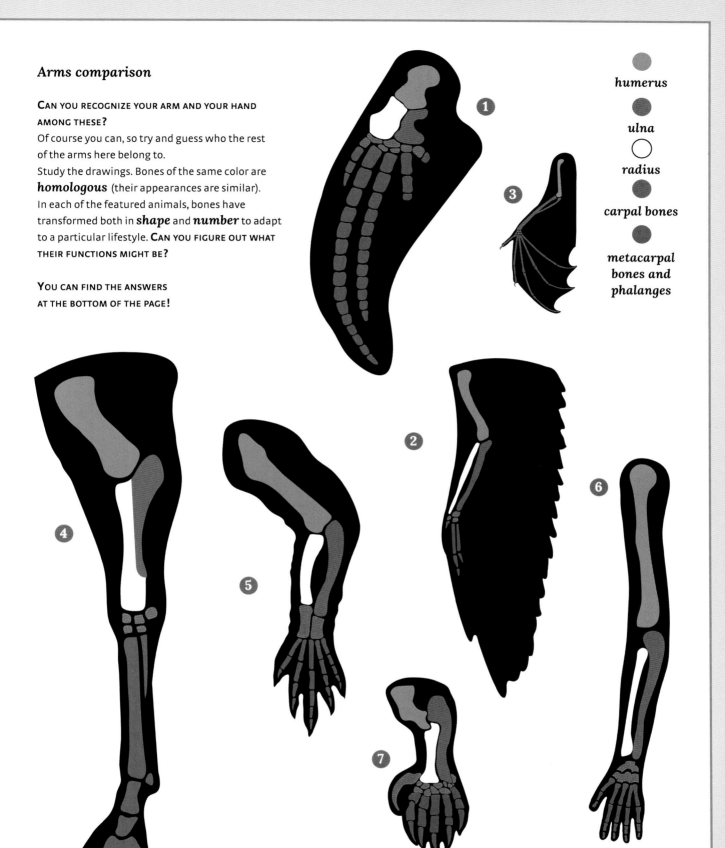

to dig 7 mole 7
to handle human 6
to run crocodile 5 — horse 4
to fly bat 3 — bird 2
to swim whale 1

19

The muscles
The engines of the body

There are almost 700 muscles in the body. They are wrapped in many layers around bones and internal organs, making up about 35-40% of our body weight. Below are the muscles. It is thanks to them that our bodies can make so many different movements. The muscles even work when you are standing still, seated, or lying down. They are also busy when you are sleeping!

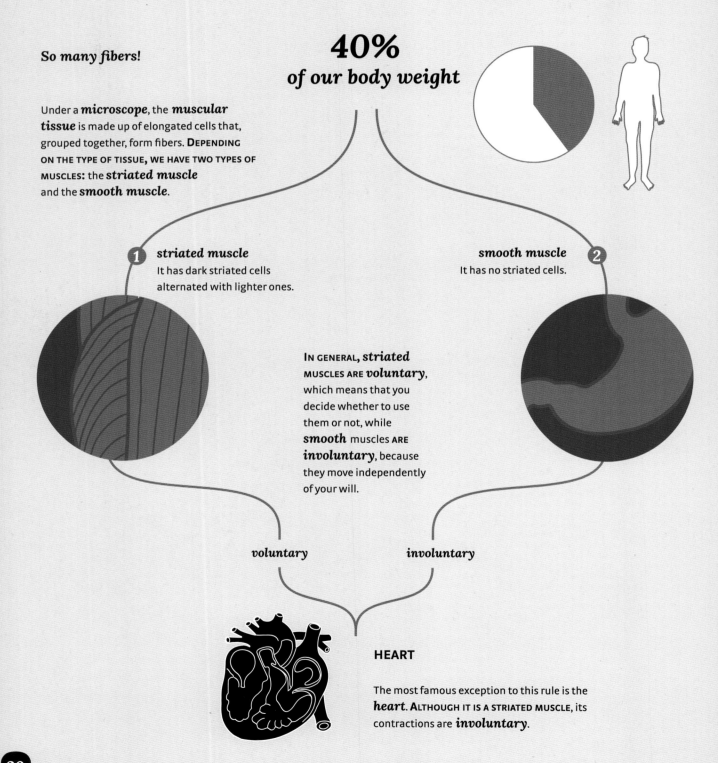

So many fibers!

Under a **microscope**, the **muscular tissue** is made up of elongated cells that, grouped together, form fibers. DEPENDING ON THE TYPE OF TISSUE, WE HAVE TWO TYPES OF MUSCLES: the **striated muscle** and the **smooth muscle**.

40%
of our body weight

1 striated muscle
It has dark striated cells alternated with lighter ones.

smooth muscle **2**
It has no striated cells.

IN GENERAL, **striated** MUSCLES ARE **voluntary**, which means that you decide whether to use them or not, while **smooth** muscles ARE **involuntary**, because they move independently of your will.

voluntary

involuntary

HEART

The most famous exception to this rule is the **heart**. ALTHOUGH IT IS A STRIATED MUSCLE, its contractions are **involuntary**.

The skeletal muscles

These muscles COLLABORATE WITH THE BONES OF THE SKELETON TO ALLOW THE BODY TO MAKE MOVEMENTS. Their fibers are **striated**. Each of these muscles has an **origin**, a **belly** (the actual muscle), and an **insertion** that almost always occurs through a **tendon**.

The properties of the muscles

contractility

the ability to contract, i.e. to become smaller

elasticity

the ability to stretch

ESOPHAGUS

STOMACH

INTESTINE

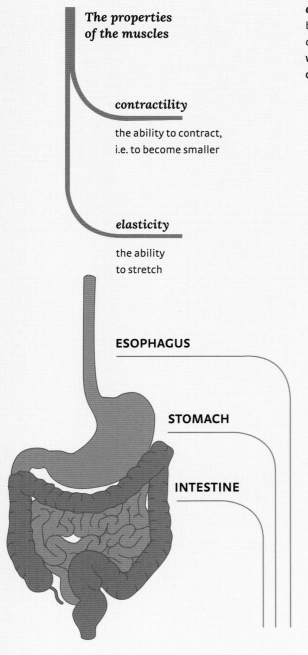

Loyal pairs

Opposite movements, such as the BENDING OR STRETCHING OF AN ARM, are performed by two different muscles, called **antagonists**, but not because they are enemies; quite the opposite. THEY WORK TOGETHER LIKE A CLOSE COUPLE!

origin

belly

insertion

Smooth muscles

The **smooth** muscles are those that YOU CAN'T CONTROL DIRECTLY. There are many of them. They are wrapped around all internal organs and make them move to a rhythm, which is necessary to keep them alive, so THEY ARE ALL VERY IMPORTANT.

IF YOU CAN SWALLOW FOOD EVEN WHEN YOU ARE UPSIDE DOWN (don't test this out, of course!), IT IS THANKS TO THE MOVEMENTS of the **involuntary muscles** along the walls of the **esophagus**, which carry the food all the way to the **stomach**, even if they have to fight against gravity.

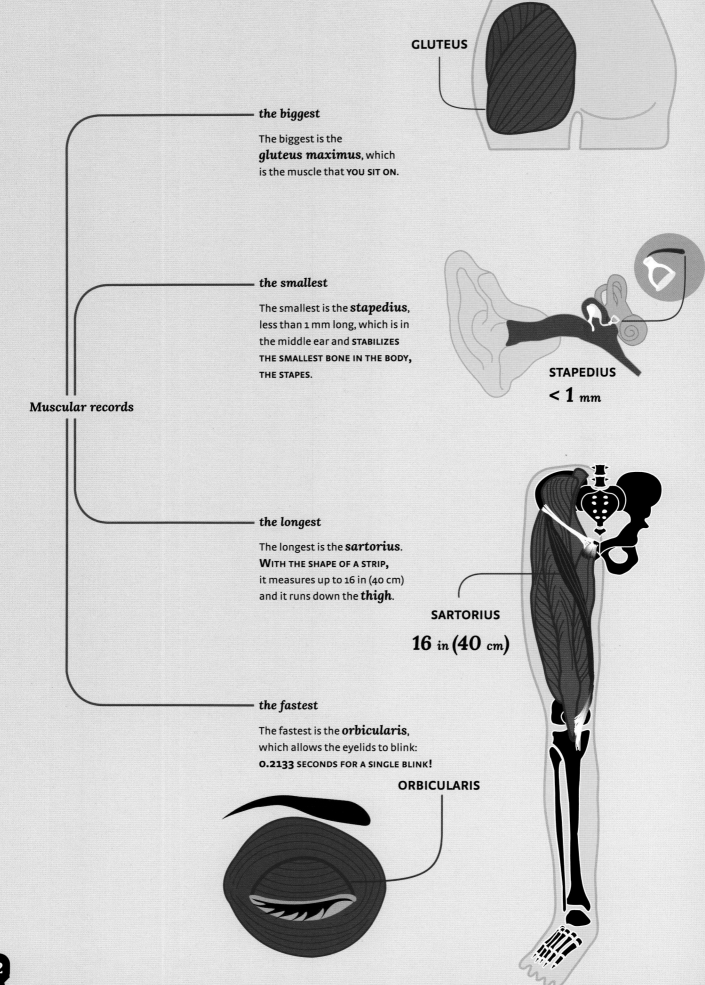

GLUTEUS

Muscular records

the biggest

The biggest is the **gluteus maximus**, which is the muscle that YOU SIT ON.

the smallest

The smallest is the **stapedius**, less than 1 mm long, which is in the middle ear and STABILIZES THE SMALLEST BONE IN THE BODY, THE STAPES.

STAPEDIUS
< 1 mm

the longest

The longest is the **sartorius**. WITH THE SHAPE OF A STRIP, it measures up to 16 in (40 cm) and it runs down the **thigh**.

SARTORIUS
16 in (40 cm)

the fastest

The fastest is the **orbicularis**, which allows the eyelids to blink: **0.2133 SECONDS FOR A SINGLE BLINK!**

ORBICULARIS

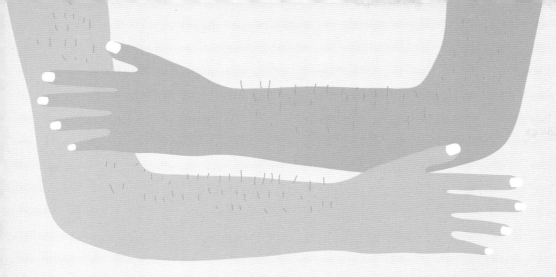

Horrifying!

Each hair has a tiny muscle at its base, which contracts and makes the hair lift up, in a bizarre action called **HORRIPILATION**. This happens when **WE FEEL COLD,** but also when we experience strong feelings such as fear or when we feel emotional. When we say we have the so-called **goose bumps**, we are actually talking about horripilation!

What faces are you making?

There is a group of muscles, called **cutaneous**, which don't move the bones, but rather the skin. It is easy to see them in action on the back of a horse, twitching to removes flies. In a human being, **THE CUTANEOUS MUSCLES ARE ONLY ON THE FACE.** There are about twenty of them, and they are called **muscles of expression**: THEY ALLOW US TO MAKE ALL THE FACIAL EXPRESSIONS WE USE TO COMMUNICATE.

A special muscle: the iris dilator

UNDER THE SUN, YOUR PUPIL CONSTRICTS down to a diameter of 0.06 in (1.5 mm), **WHILE IN THE SHADE IT CAN DILATE** up to 0.3 in (8 mm). These changes are governed by a tiny, yet complex, system of **smooth muscles**.

Brrrr, it's so cold!

DO YOU KNOW WHAT SHIVERING IS? It is a defense against the cold. The action is the result of dozens of **MUSCLES CONTRACTING AND RELEASING EXTREMELY RAPIDLY TO INCREASE OUR BODY TEMPERATURE.** Another function of muscular contraction is to generate warmth. For this reason, it is a crucial form of protection for the body. Isn't it true that, when you work your muscles, you feel hot? Or that, when you feel cold, you have a natural impulse to clap your hands and hop?

constricted pupil   dilated pupil

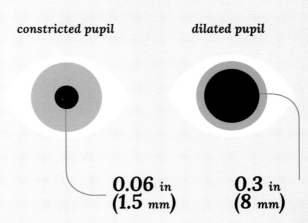

0.06 in (1.5 mm)   **0.3 in (8 mm)**

Electric fish

EVERY TIME A MUSCLE CONTRACTS, IT GENERATES A SMALL ELECTRIC SHOCK. This shock is so weak that it doesn't give us any discomfort.

Some fish have developed muscular fibers that are bigger than normal, with **electric potentials** way greater than the ones normally needed to make muscles function. These modified muscular cells are called **electrocytes,** and they can emit electric discharges into the surrounding water.

The most famous electric fish are the **electric ray** and other fish similar to eels. They say that the electric fish commonly known as the **electric eel** can generate a shock of **600 volts** – ALMOST THREE TIMES THE VOLTAGE USED IN HOUSES!

There are about 400 species of fish with the ability to "give an electric shock."

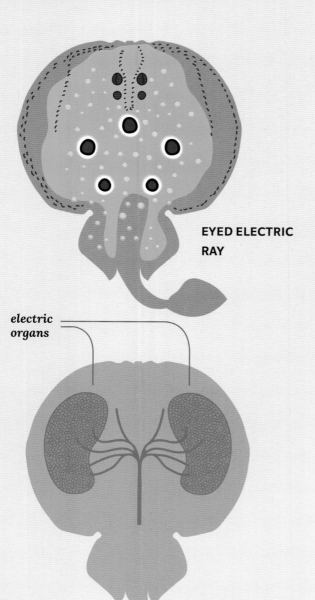

EYED ELECTRIC RAY

electric organs

ELECTRIC EEL

600 volts!

A muscly...day

CONNECT THE WORDS AND PHRASES IN THE SHORT STORIES TO THE VARIOUS MUSCLES
THAT ARE ACTIVATED (SEE BELOW).
YOU CAN FIND THE SOLUTIONS AT THE BOTTOM OF THE PAGE!

1 It is a nice spring morning. Mom wakes Marco up to go to school. He opens his eyes. When his mom pulls the blinds, **the sunlight hits him** in the face.

2 Marco **sits up in the bed** and eventually gets up.

3 After getting himself washed, dressed, and fed, **he lifts his backpack up from the floor** and goes to school.

4 Halfway through the morning, there is a break. This is lucky, because Marco was starting to feel hungry. He takes his sandwich out of his backpack and **eats it with purpose**.

5 He enjoys the sandwich, unlike the spinach served for lunch, which he **swallows** with a lot of effort.

6 In the afternoon, Marco has soccer practice. He plays offense. After a few minutes, **he kicks the ball hard** and it flies into the net – his first goal! In the audience, his friend Alice sits. She has blonde hair with braids.

7 8 He is a bit in love with her...

9 Alice **lifts her arms in victory,** and Marco **gets very excited**.
Before going to bed, Marco looks out his bedroom window. **He lifts his head** and looks up.
Wow, there is a big, full moon lighting up the whole garden!

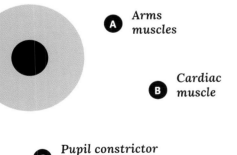
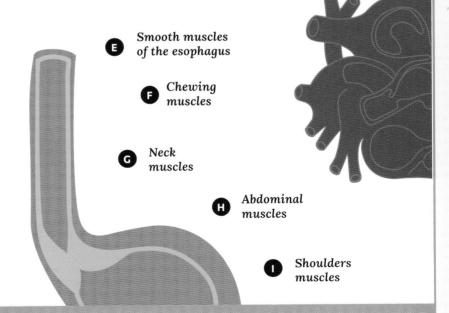

A Arms muscles

B Cardiac muscle

C Pupil constrictor muscle

D Leg muscles

E Smooth muscles of the esophagus

F Chewing muscles

G Neck muscles

H Abdominal muscles

I Shoulders muscles

G 6 · B 8 · I 7 · D 6 · E 5 · F 4 · A 3 · H 2 · C 1 · G 9

25

The skin

The body "coat"

If you were asked to name an organ of the human body, the stomach, heart, lungs or brain would most likely come to mind. It might never occur to you to think about the skin. The skin is actually an organ just like all the others, with its own specific structure and precise functions.

It is the **largest** organ, and also the **heaviest**. In a man of average build, THE SKIN COVERS A SURFACE OF **21.5** SQUARE FEET (**2** SQUARE METERS) and weighs about 22 lb (10 kg).
That's almost 15% of the body weight!

A very resistant organ

Among our organs, the skin is also the **most resistant**. A 0.4 in (1 cm) long strip of skin, about 0.12 in (3 mm) thick, can bear a weight of up to 22 lb (10 kg), just like a small suitcase. THE SKIN STRETCHES LIKE AN ELASTIC BAND!

The human skin weighs about

22 lb (10 kg)

and makes up almost

15%

of the body weight

0.4 in (1 cm)

0.12 in (3 mm)

What is the purpose of the skin?

Its first function is to **protect**. The skin is a true barrier against dust, microbes, and harmful substances that could penetrate into the body.

At the same time, it prevents the water that is necessary to make the body function from coming out, thus avoiding **dehydration**.

thickness of the palm of a hand

0.06 in (1.5 cm)

The skin also serves the purpose of **softening impacts**. If you get hurt, you might see a **bruise** forming, but the muscles and bones underneath don't get seriously damaged.

Functions of the skin

PROTECT

ELIMINATE WASTE

SENSATION (TOUCH)

The sweat

Another important task of the skin is to **ELIMINATE PART OF THE WASTE PRODUCED BY THE BODY** through *sweat*. That's why sweating is important, even if it can be uncomfortable sometimes...

When you rest, even if you don't realize it, you can produce more than 2.1 pt (1 l) of sweat per night. If you are exercising, you can make over 21 pt (10 l)!

thickness of an eyelid

0.02 mm

Thanks to specific cells inside the skin, called *receptors*, YOU CAN FEEL HOT, COLD, PAIN, ETC. BY TOUCHING AN OBJECT, YOU CAN ALSO UNDERSTAND IF IT'S SOFT, HARD, FLAT, OR ROUGH.

The skin hosts one of the five senses: touch.

Layers of coat

The layer of the *epidermis* is in contact with the external world and is made up of dead cells. ABOUT 30 THOUSAND SKIN CELLS DIE EVERY MINUTE. They come off and are replaced by *new ones*. WITHIN A MONTH, THE WHOLE OUTER LAYER IS COMPLETELY RENEWED.

During our lifetimes, we lose up to 44 lb (20 kg) of skin!

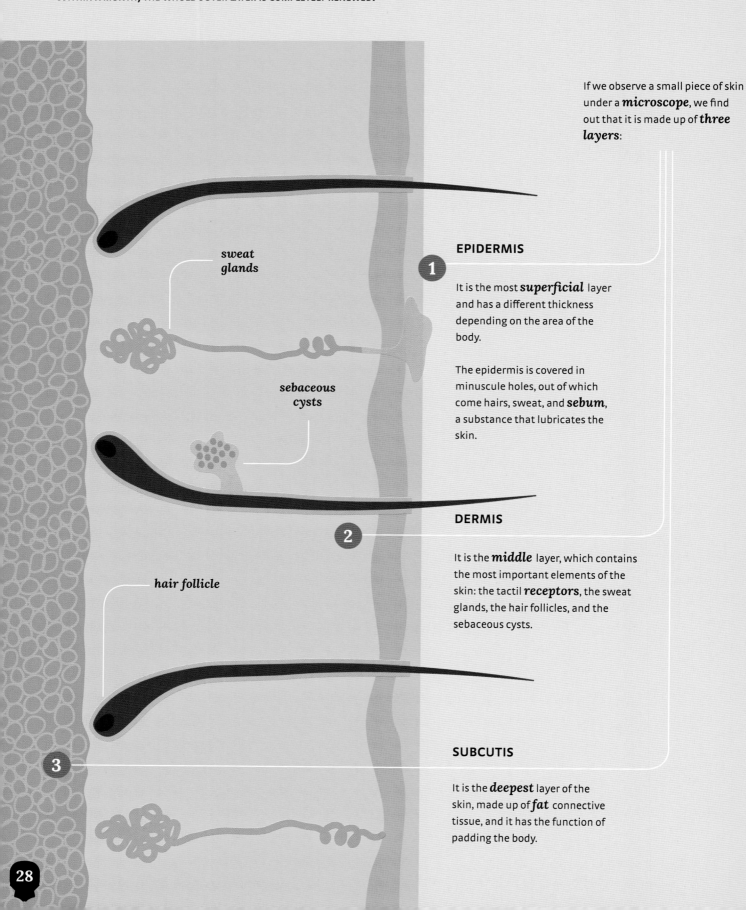

If we observe a small piece of skin under a **microscope**, we find out that it is made up of **three layers**:

sweat glands

sebaceous cysts

hair follicle

1 **EPIDERMIS**

It is the most **superficial** layer and has a different thickness depending on the area of the body.

The epidermis is covered in minuscule holes, out of which come hairs, sweat, and **sebum**, a substance that lubricates the skin.

2 **DERMIS**

It is the **middle** layer, which contains the most important elements of the skin: the tactil **receptors**, the sweat glands, the hair follicles, and the sebaceous cysts.

3 **SUBCUTIS**

It is the **deepest** layer of the skin, made up of **fat** connective tissue, and it has the function of padding the body.

The cutaneous annexes: hair and nails

Hairs grow all over the body except for the LIPS, the **palms of the hands,** and the **soles of the feet**.

our nails grow
on average
0.04 in (1 mm)
every 10 days

A single hair can
hold the **weight
of an apple!**

Our hair grows
on average
0.4 in
(1 cm) a month

The colors of skin and hair

Depending on the person, the **complexion** can be very fair
or very dark, with a lot of shades between.
The same can be said for **hair**. We can have light blonde,
almost white hair, or pitch black hair. Red and brown hair
are shades which land in the middle.

The melanin protects
the skin from the
ultraviolet rays of the sun.

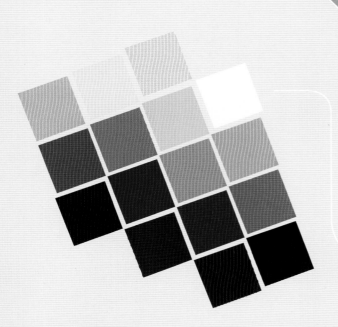

All these
different
shades depend
on the presence of
a colored pigment in
the skin, called **melanin**,
which each person has in
different quantities. WHEN YOU
HAVE ONLY A LITTLE, YOU ARE PALE, BUT
WHEN YOU TAN, YOUR EPIDERMIS PRODUCES
MORE OF IT AND BECOMES DARKER.

In elderly people, the **whiteness** of the hair is
caused by a lack of melanin. But that's not all – if
it was just for the melanin, the hair would be...
trasparent. The melanin is replaced by tiny air
bubbles that diffuse and reflect the light, just like
what happens with foam soap. The bubbles make
the hair look white.

29

What about animals?

A human has the same number of hairs as a chimpanzee. They both have about 5 million hair follicles.

The naked monkey

If this is true, then why do monkeys look hairier then humans? And why do humans have the nickname "*naked monkeys?*"
BECAUSE MOST HUMAN HAIRS ARE SO SHORT, FAIR, AND THIN THAT THEY ARE ALMOST INVISIBLE TO THE NAKED EYE.

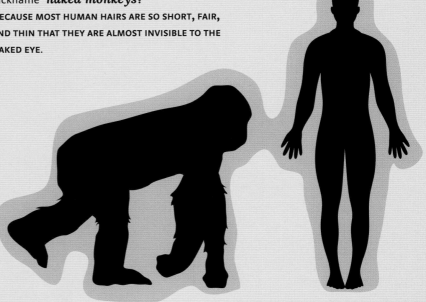

DO YOU KNOW WHAT **"pachyderm"** MEANS? It's a word that comes from Greek and means **thick skin**. The skin of a pachyderm like the **rhinoceros** can be as thick as 2 in (5 cm). Elephant skin is just as thick!

Despite its thickness, pachyderm skin remains as sensitive as ours.

thickness of the skin

2 in (5 cm)

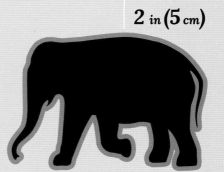

The bodies of most **mammals** are covered in hairs. However, there are some that have none, like **dolphins** and **whales**. This is because these animals live in water, and hairs would only be a hindrance.

Instead of hairs, which only mammals have, **fish** and **reptiles** have **scales**, while **birds** have **feathers** and **down**. **Frogs** and **toads**, like all amphibians, have "**naked**" skin.

hairs
MAMMALS

few hairs
AQUATIC MAMMALS

Different animals, different coats

scales
FISH AND REPTILES

What does the color depend on?

The **melanin** is the main pigment of the skin in mammals, but there are some colors in animals that come from other pigments.
The **carotenoids**, PRESENT IN THE VEGETABLES THAT BIRDS EAT, are responsible for coloring the feathers in **red** and **yellow**.

feathers and down
BIRDS

naked skin
AMPHIBIANS

The **light or deep blue color** of certain animals is not created by a pigment, it's a "**trick.**" Thanks to their particular structures, the skin of a **mandrill**'s face and the feathers of a parrot **scatter the light**, like the sky does, and appear to be blue.

MANDRILL

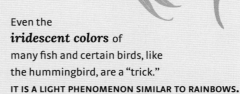

Even the **iridescent colors** of many fish and certain birds, like the hummingbird, are a "trick."
IT IS A LIGHT PHENOMENON SIMILAR TO RAINBOWS.

The blood

A liquid tissue

It feels impossible to imagine the blood as a tissue, but that's what it is: it belongs to the connective tissues.

THE BLOOD HAS ALL THE CHARACTERISTICS TYPICAL OF A TISSUE because it is made up of specialized cells that carry out specific functions. The difference between blood and other tissues is that its cells are immersed in a liquid called *plasma*, which allows blood to flow uninterruptedly during our lifetimes. The blood flows along *vessels* that transport it to all parts of the body.

55%
plasma

0.1%
white blood cells

2.6%
platelets

42.3%
red blood cells

The composition of blood

Plasma, the LIQUID PART of the blood, comprises 55% of the total. This means that the FORMED ELEMENTS, i.e. the cells that are in the plasma, make up for 45%.

WHAT ARE THE FORMED ELEMENTS AND HOW ARE THEY DIFFERENT?

If you know your weight, you can calculate how much blood is in your body: about 2.1 pt (1 l) for every 29 lb (13 kg) of weight.

The blood cells

The shapes and dimensions of blood cells are very different from one another. Most of them are produced in the **bone marrow**, which has a huge reserve of immature cells, called **stem cells**.
The marrow produces BETWEEN 150 AND 200 BILLION RED BLOOD CELLS AND PLATELETS EVERY DAY, ALONG WITH TENS OF BILLIONS OF WHITE BLOOD CELLS.

red blood cell

The average life span of a red blood cell is about 4 months. During that period, it travels almost 930 miles (1,500 km).

The white blood cells or leucocytes

The white blood cells are **our defense** against potential "enemies." There are different types, and each one of them **uses a different strategy** to fight and defeat bacteria, viruses, and other harmful microrganisms that try to penetrate our bodies. SOME OF THEM ENGULF THE ENEMY, INGEST IT, AND "DIGEST IT." THIS IS A PROCESS CALLED "PHAGOCYTOSIS."

Other white blood cells use more refined systems. They produce the famous **antibodies**, which are different for each disease.

Types of white blood cells

white blood cell

The platelets

platelet

THE PLATELETS ARE THE SMALLEST ELEMENTS OF THE BLOOD because they are not real cells. They are instead PIECES OF BIG CELLS, called **megakaryocytes**, which are formed in the bone marrow like blood cells but tend to break up.

The platelets might appear insignificant at first, but they are in fact **fundamental** in the complex process of BLOOD COAGULATION. Their function is to clump every time you have a **scratch** or a **cut**. They gather at the wound and, along with red blood cells, they form a **clot** that stops the bleeding.

The red blood cells (or erythrocytes)

The shape of a human **red blood cell** is unmistakable. Take a small ball of red clay and squeeze it between your thumb and index finger. **YOU'VE JUST CREATED A GIGANTIC ERYTHROCYTE!**

In truth, the red blood cells of a human are **VERY SMALL** — among the smallest, actually; they measure between **6 and 8 microns** (remember that one meter corresponds to one million microns). The average size of many other cells is between 30 and 40 microns.

Red like iron

The red color of the eryhtrocytes is provided by **hemoglobin**, a **PROTEIN THAT CONTAINS IRON**. Each erythrocyte contains **270 million molecules** of hemoglobin! In order to make room for such a huge quantity of molecules in such a tiny cell, red blood cells don't have nuclei or other common organelles.

Why is hemoglobin so important? Because it carries oxygen and transports it to all cells in the body. Cells need this oxygen to survive.

A redder blood

HUMAN POPULATIONS LIVING AT HIGH ALTITUDES BETWEEN 9,800 and 13,000 ft (3,000-4,000 m) HAVE A HIGHER COUNT OF RED BLOOD CELLS COMPARED TO OTHER POPULATIONS. This is because air at those altitudes is **poorer in oxygen** and the only way to have the necessary quantity reaching all cells is to ... **ADD MORE HEMOGLOBIN!**

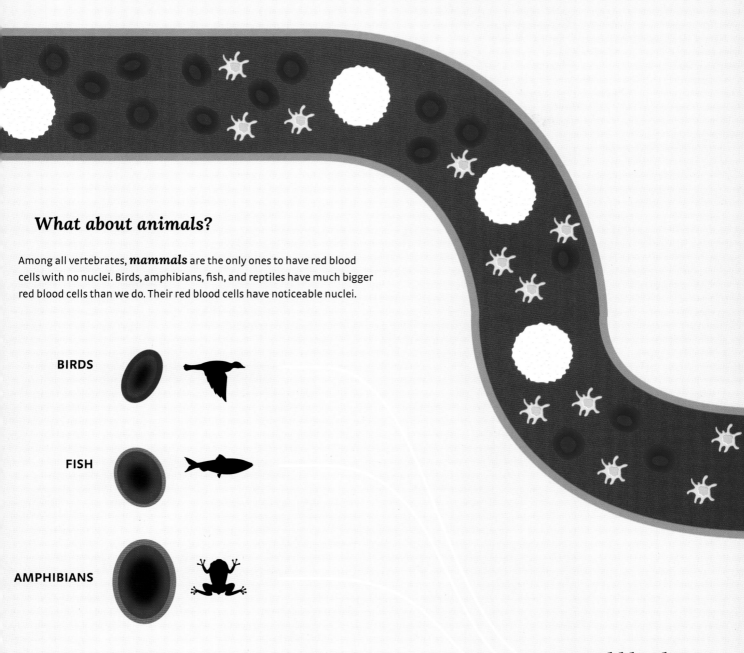

What about animals?

Among all vertebrates, **mammals** are the only ones to have red blood cells with no nuclei. Birds, amphibians, fish, and reptiles have much bigger red blood cells than we do. Their red blood cells have noticeable nuclei.

BIRDS

FISH

AMPHIBIANS

REPTILES

red blood cells in other animals

Living without red blood cells

THERE IS ONE VERTEBRATE WITH NO RED BLOOD CELLS IN ITS BLOOD: the **crocodile icefish** (*Chionodraco hamatus*). This fish lives in the cold Antarctic waters, which are very rich in oxygen. THE OXYGEN PASSES THROUGH THE GILLS INTO THE BLOOD, WHERE IT TRAVELS FREELY without needing hemoglobin to transport it.

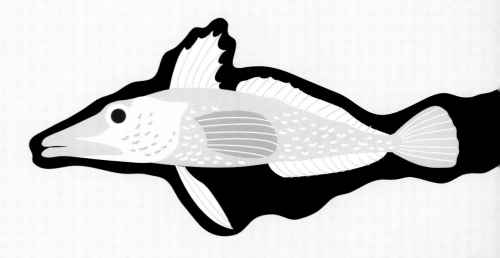

The heart and the vascular system

The beat of life

The blood flow is called "the stream of life." Like the water in a stream, the blood flows, but a stream eventually flows into a bigger river or the sea. Blood flows in a circulatory way, completing the same journey over and over again. That's why we call it blood circulation.

The heart

Our most important muscle, the **heart**, is situated inside the ribcage and between our two **lungs**. It works as a HANDLING CENTER FOR THE VASCULAR SYSTEM. Inside the heart are **four chambers** – two atria and two ventricles.

INSIDE THE HEART, THE BLOOD CAN FLOW ONLY IN ONE DIRECTION. IT ENTERS FROM THE ATRIA AND COMES OUT THROUGH THE VENTRICLES. Thanks to specific valves, which open to let the blood in and close immediately afterwards, the blood cannot reverse its course.

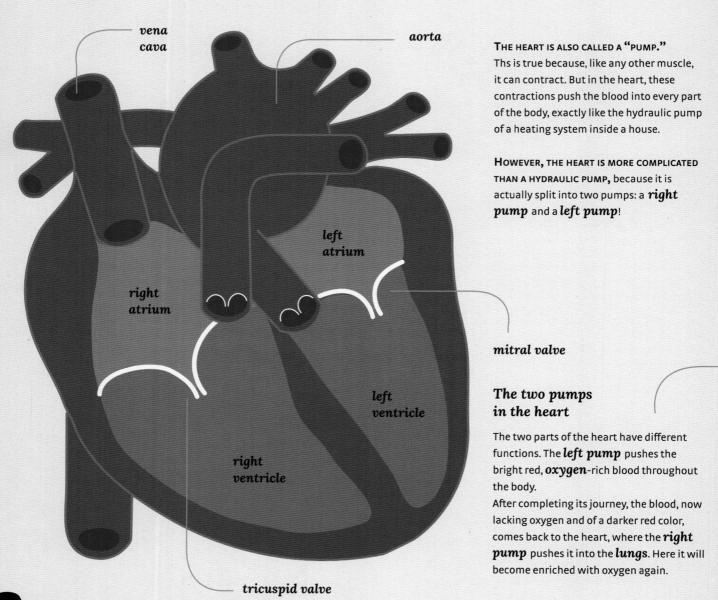

vena cava

aorta

left atrium

right atrium

mitral valve

left ventricle

right ventricle

tricuspid valve

THE HEART IS ALSO CALLED A "PUMP." Ths is true because, like any other muscle, it can contract. But in the heart, these contractions push the blood into every part of the body, exactly like the hydraulic pump of a heating system inside a house.

HOWEVER, THE HEART IS MORE COMPLICATED THAN A HYDRAULIC PUMP, because it is actually split into two pumps: a **right pump** and a **left pump**!

The two pumps in the heart

The two parts of the heart have different functions. The **left pump** pushes the bright red, **oxygen**-rich blood throughout the body.
After completing its journey, the blood, now lacking oxygen and of a darker red color, comes back to the heart, where the **right pump** pushes it into the **lungs**. Here it will become enriched with oxygen again.

Arteries, veins, and capillaries

The vessels through which the blood travels, called **blood vessels**, have different names depending on their structures, dimensions, and "senses of direction."
The **arteries** are the vessels that originate from the heart, carrying blood to the whole body. THE FURTHER AWAY THEY GET FROM THE HEART, THE THINNER THEY BECOME, UNTIL THEY REACH THE DIMENSIONS OF A HAIR. Now the vessels are called **capillaries**.
From the capillaries, the blood starts its journey back through the **veins**, which are the vessels that connect back to the heart.

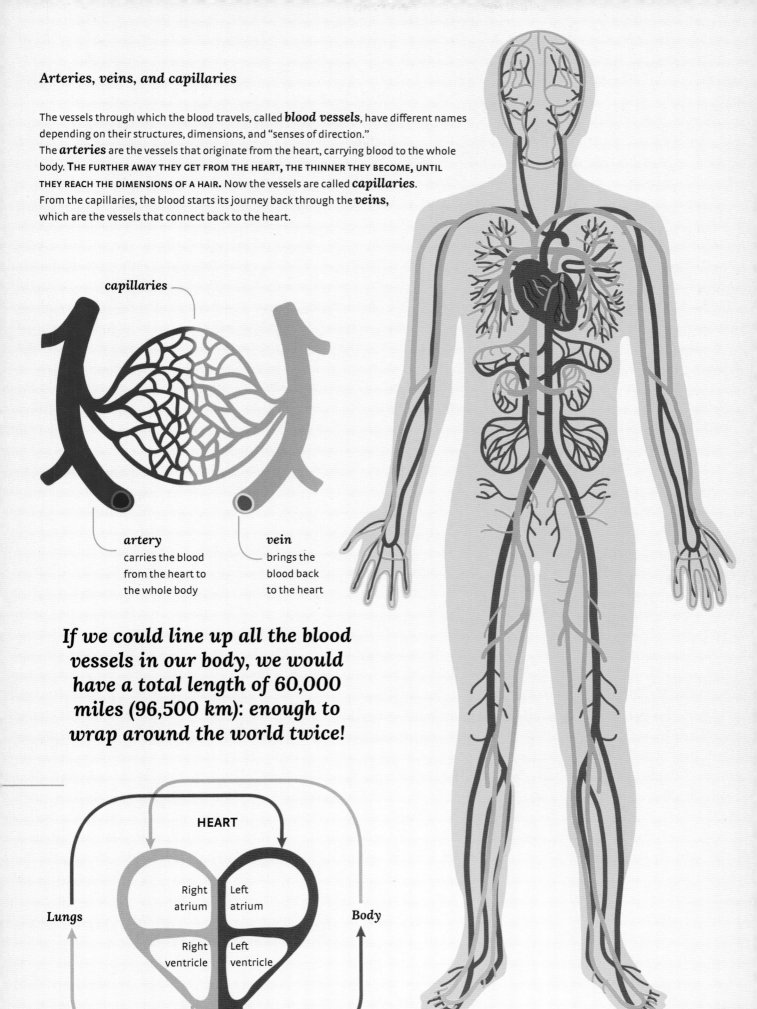

capillaries

artery
carries the blood
from the heart to
the whole body

vein
brings the
blood back
to the heart

If we could line up all the blood vessels in our body, we would have a total length of 60,000 miles (96,500 km): enough to wrap around the world twice!

HEART

Right
atrium

Left
atrium

Lungs

Body

Right
ventricle

Left
ventricle

What about animals?

WHY DO WE SAY THAT OUR CIRCULATION IS DOUBLE AND COMPLETE?

Our circulation is **double** because our **BLOOD PASSES THROUGH THE HEART TWICE**. It is **complete** because **THE BLOOD RICH IN OXYGEN AND THE BLOOD POOR IN OXYGEN NEVER MIX**. This type of circulation is not unique to human beings, as it can be found in **mammals** and **birds**.

Reptiles and **amphibians** have double circulation too, but it is incomplete. Their hearts have two atria, but only one ventricle, so the oxygenated blood mixes with the non-oxygenated blood. The situation is different for **fish**, because these animals have no lungs. The blood oxygenates in the gills. From there, it reaches the rest of the body, traveling through the heart only once.
THAT'S WHY WE SAY THAT FISH HAVE SIMPLE CIRCULATION.

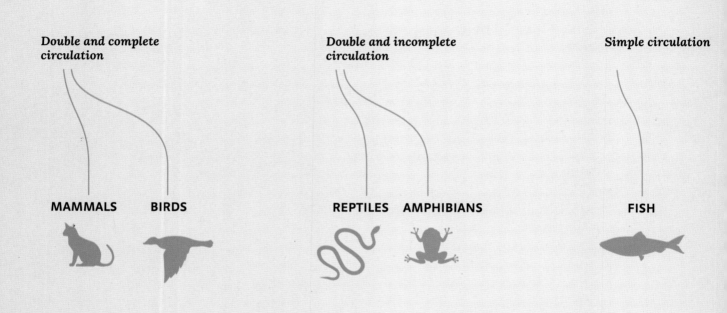

Double and complete circulation

MAMMALS   BIRDS

Double and incomplete circulation

REPTILES   AMPHIBIANS

Simple circulation

FISH

The biggest heart

WHO HAS THE BIGGEST HEART OF THEM ALL?
The **blue whale,** of course!
Its heart is almost **450 lb (200 kg).** That's nearly as big and heavy as a small piano!

diameter
12 in (30 cm)

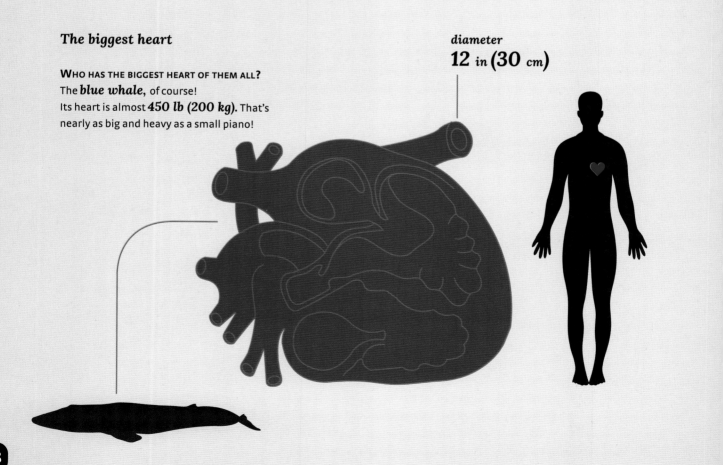

The heart beat

If you put your ear against one of your friends' chests, you should be able to hear their heart beat. WHAT EXACTLY PRODUCES THIS SOUND? It is the NOISE MADE BY THE VALVES OF THE HEART CLOSING. In human beings, the cardiac frequency is about **70-90 beats** *per minute* (when at rest), but it is higher in children (between **100 and 120 beats**). On average, throughout our lives, the heart is estimated to beat at least *three billion times*!

WHAT IS THE CARDIAC FREQUENCY IN OTHER ANIMALS?

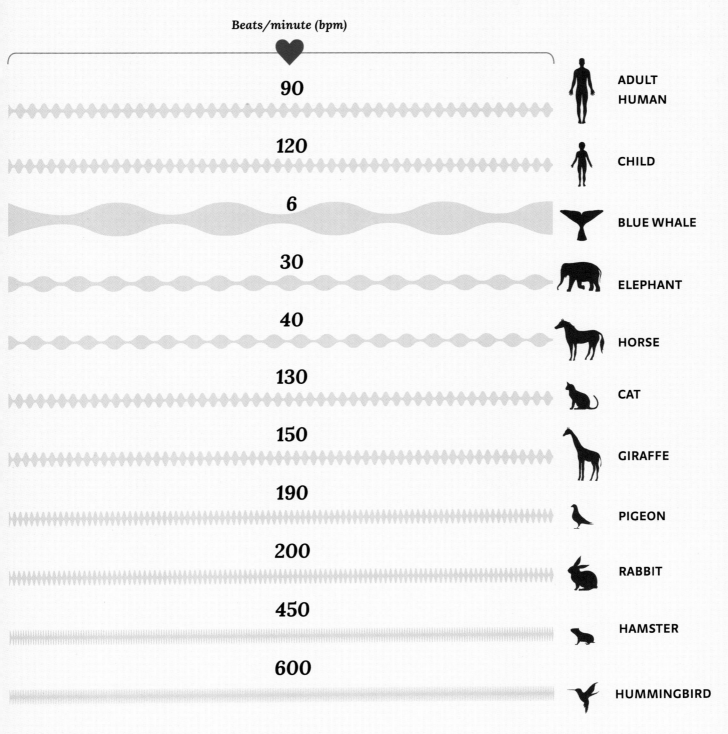

Beats/minute (bpm)

bpm	Animal
90	ADULT HUMAN
120	CHILD
6	BLUE WHALE
30	ELEPHANT
40	HORSE
130	CAT
150	GIRAFFE
190	PIGEON
200	RABBIT
450	HAMSTER
600	HUMMINGBIRD

During a fight between male hummingbirds, the cardiac frequencies of the birds can reach over 1,000 beats per minute - a record in the animal kingdom!

The lungs

Breath of fresh air

Holding your breath for too long, for instance when swimming underwater, can be dangerous. The body needs a continuous supply of oxygen, which is essential for survival. The body also needs to continuously expel the toxic gas carbon dioxide, which is the waste produced by the cells in the body.

Each breath is made up of two phases: the **inhalation**, when we take in the air, and the **exhalation**, when we expel it.

O_2 (oxygen)

CO_2 (carbon dioxide)

The breathing

When you are at rest, you take about **15 breaths a minute**. When you were born, you breathed at a higher frequency: **up to 70 times a minute**!

With each inhalation, you introduce 1 pt (half a l) of air into your body and therefore 12–17 pt (6–8 l) per minute.

15 breaths a minute

When entering the body, the air follows a precise route through the **nose** or **mouth** (or both). It then goes into the **throat**, the **trachea**, and the **2 bronchi**, which then branch out into the **2 lungs**. Upon exhaling, the route is the same, but in the opposite direction.

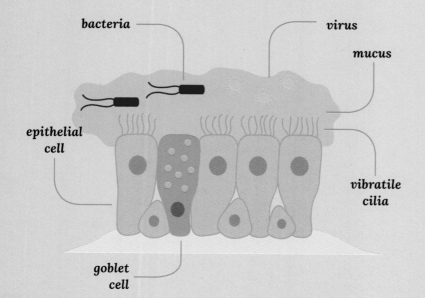

bacteria

virus

mucus

epithelial cell

vibratile cilia

goblet cell

Natural purifiers

THE AIR WE BREATHE ALWAYS CONTAINS FOREIGN PARTICLES such as dust, pollen, or microbes (no matter if we're in the city or a clean forest). These particles must not reach the lungs. They are **blocked** in the airways by the **mucus**, a dense and sticky substance, and are then swept away by the **cilia**.
A COUGH, which is a violent and noisy exhalation, SERVES EXACTLY THIS PURPOSE OF HELPING OUR RESPIRATORY SYSTEMS GET RID OF HARMFUL SUBSTANCES THAT NEED TO BE ELIMINATED.

The lungs

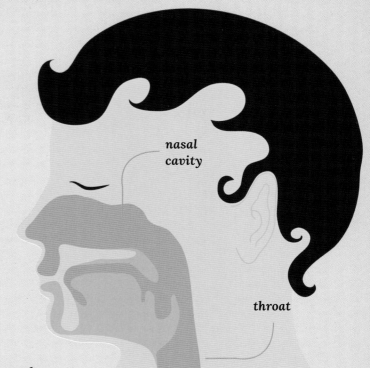

THE LUNGS LOOK LIKE TWO BIG, CONICAL SACS.
THEY ARE PROTECTED BY THE RIBCAGE.
Their **spongy** textures are due to the incredible
amount of tiny air sacs, or **alveoli**, which are placed
at the extremities of the smallest branches of the
bronchi. If you can believe it, their total count in
both lungs is between **400 and 700 milion**.
It is through the walls of the alveoli that the gases are
exchanged, meaning oxygen is passed into the blood
and the blood releases the carbon dioxide to expel.
If we added up the measurements of the internal
surfaces of all the alveoli, we would have almost **2,100
square feet (200 square meters)**, or a bit less
than the surface of a tennis court!

nasal cavity

throat

trachea

primary bronchi

lungs

diaphragm

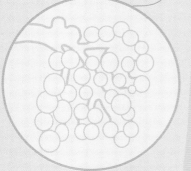

Every day, during regular
exchanges in the blood,
red blood cells absorb
almost **8,000 pt
(200 l) of oxygen**
and leave behind
**1,000 pt (500 l)
of carbon dioxide**.

No diaphragm, no breathing

The **lungs** don't have muscular tissue,
SO THEY CAN'T MOVE ON THEIR OWN.
That's why their bases rest on top a very
important muscle, the **diaphragm**.
WHEN INHALING, THE DIAPHRAGM
CONTRACTS AND DROPS, LEAVING ROOM FOR
THE LUNGS TO EXPAND. WHEN EXHALING,
THE DIAPHRAGM RELAXES AND LIFTS UP
AGAIN, HELPING THE LUNGS PUSH AIR OUT.

What about animals?

ALL OTHER MAMMALS HAVE LUNGS SIMILAR TO OURS, AND THEIR BREATHING WORKS THE SAME WAY. THERE IS ONE EXCEPTION: the *cetaceans*. *Dolphins*, *whales*, and *sperm whales* don't breathe automatically. THEY HAVE TO DECIDE WHEN TO DO IT. This is possible for these animals because THEY STORE A HUGE RESERVE OF OXYGEN IN THEIR BLOOD AND MUSCLES. They can thus afford to breathe more infrequently.

A sperm whale can stay underwater without breathing for almost two hours!

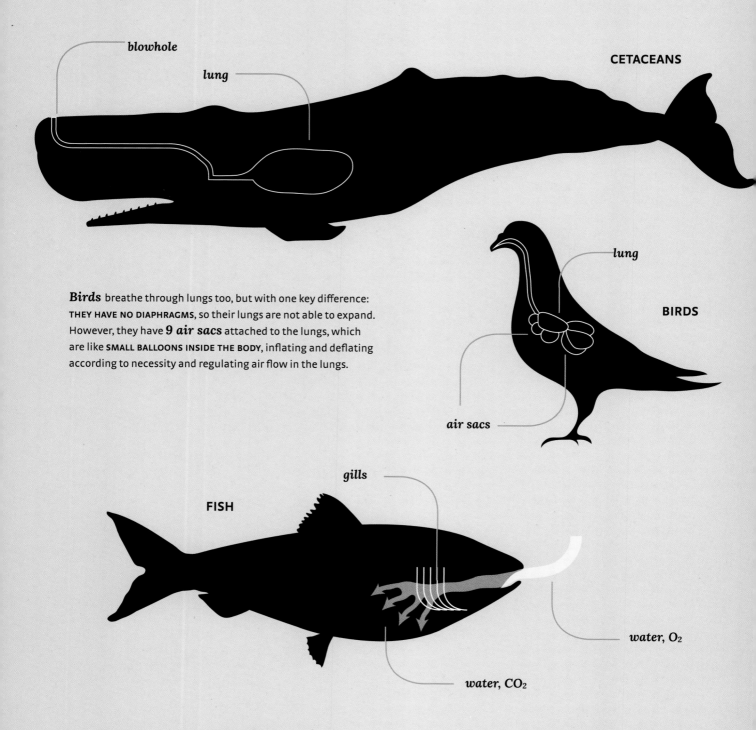

blowhole

lung

CETACEANS

lung

BIRDS

air sacs

gills

FISH

water, O_2

water, CO_2

Birds breathe through lungs too, but with one key difference: THEY HAVE NO DIAPHRAGMS, so their lungs are not able to expand. However, they have **9 *air sacs*** attached to the lungs, which are like SMALL BALLOONS INSIDE THE BODY, inflating and deflating according to necessity and regulating air flow in the lungs.

There is a group of vertebrates, the *fish*, that don't have lungs at all. The reason is obvious: because they live in water, they can't breathe air. However, like us, THEY NEED OXYGEN AND HAVE TO EXPEL CARBON DIOXIDE.

The gas exchange happens through specific passages at the sides of the head, called the **gills**. These are a series of **comb-like lamellae**, covered in **capillaries** that capture the oxygen in the water.

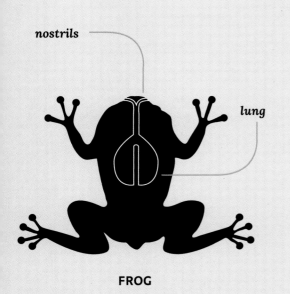

nostrils

lung

FROG

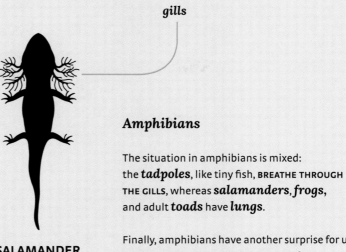

gills

SALAMANDER
LARVAE

Amphibians

The situation in amphibians is mixed:
the *tadpoles*, like tiny fish, BREATHE THROUGH
THE GILLS, whereas *salamanders*, *frogs*,
and adult *toads* have *lungs*.

Finally, amphibians have another surprise for us:
THEY CAN BREATHE THROUGH THE SKIN!

BREATHING FREQUENCY IN ANIMALS
Breath/minute

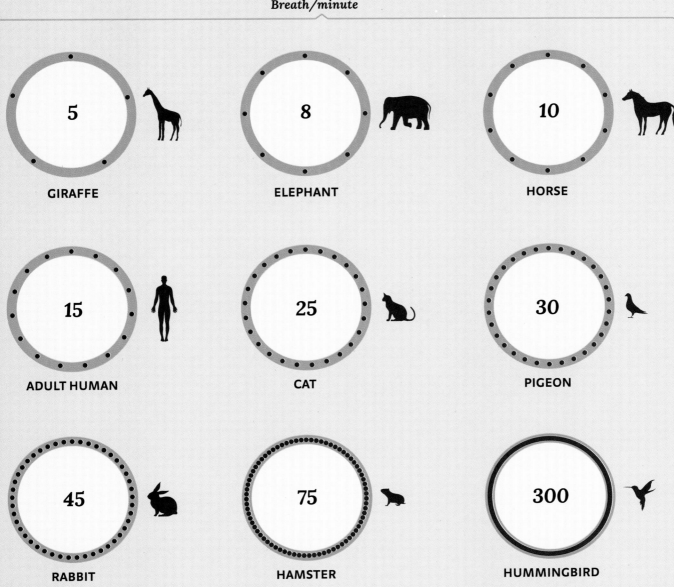

5	8	10
GIRAFFE	ELEPHANT	HORSE
15	25	30
ADULT HUMAN	CAT	PIGEON
45	75	300
RABBIT	HAMSTER	HUMMINGBIRD

The digestive system

Eat and you'll feel better

We can't survive without eating, just like how we can't survive without breathing. The reason is that each cell in the body needs energy to function. This energy comes from the nutrients that we absorb through the food we eat.

The gastrointestinal tract

Our body has a long tube that starts with the **mouth** and ends with the **anus.** Some sections are larger, some are narrower, and others are tightly folded. **This tube is called the gastrointestinal tract.**

WHAT WE EAT IS PROCESSED AND TRANSFERRED INTO THE BLOOD, WHICH THEN TAKES THE NUTRIENTS TO THE CELLS. Food makes a real JOURNEY INSIDE THE BODY!

The beginning of the journey

In order to be swallowed, a mouthful of food must be broken down and chewed by the teeth and also **moistened** by the **saliva,** a liquid produced by the **salivary glands.** These glands are situated in the **neck** and the mouth area.
At this stage, the mouthful of food is called **bolus** and is pushed by the **tongue** down the first part of the gastrointestinal tract, the **esophagus**, to start its journey.

In a single day, we can produce up to 2 pt (1 l) of saliva!

The esophagus

The **esophagus** is the first part of the **gastrointestinal tract**. It measures 10-12 in (25-30 cm) long and 0.8-1.2 in (2-3 cm) wide, and it goes from the throat to the stomach. THE BOLUS TAKES APPROXIMATELY 7 SECONDS TO PASS THROUGH IT.

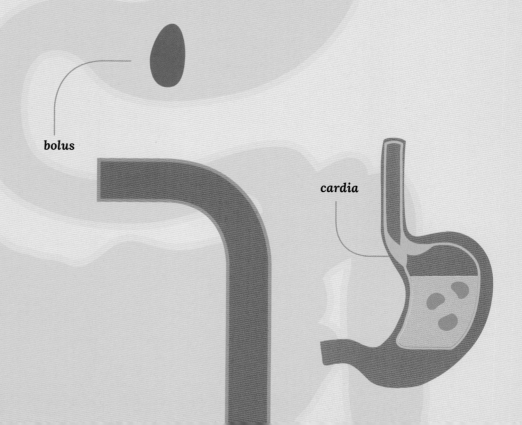

bolus

cardia

The stomach

After the esophagus is the **stomach**, the sac-like part of the digestive system that can contain up to **3 PT (1.5 L) OF FOOD.**

THE WALLS OF THE STOMACH ARE COVERED IN MUSCULAR FIBERS. As soon as the bolus of food arrives in the stomach, the fibers start contracting. **Liquids** are needed for the fibers to function, just like in the process of kneading dough.
The stomach itself produces **gastric juices,** SECRETIONS WHICH ARE MORE ACIDIC THAN LEMON OR VINEGAR.

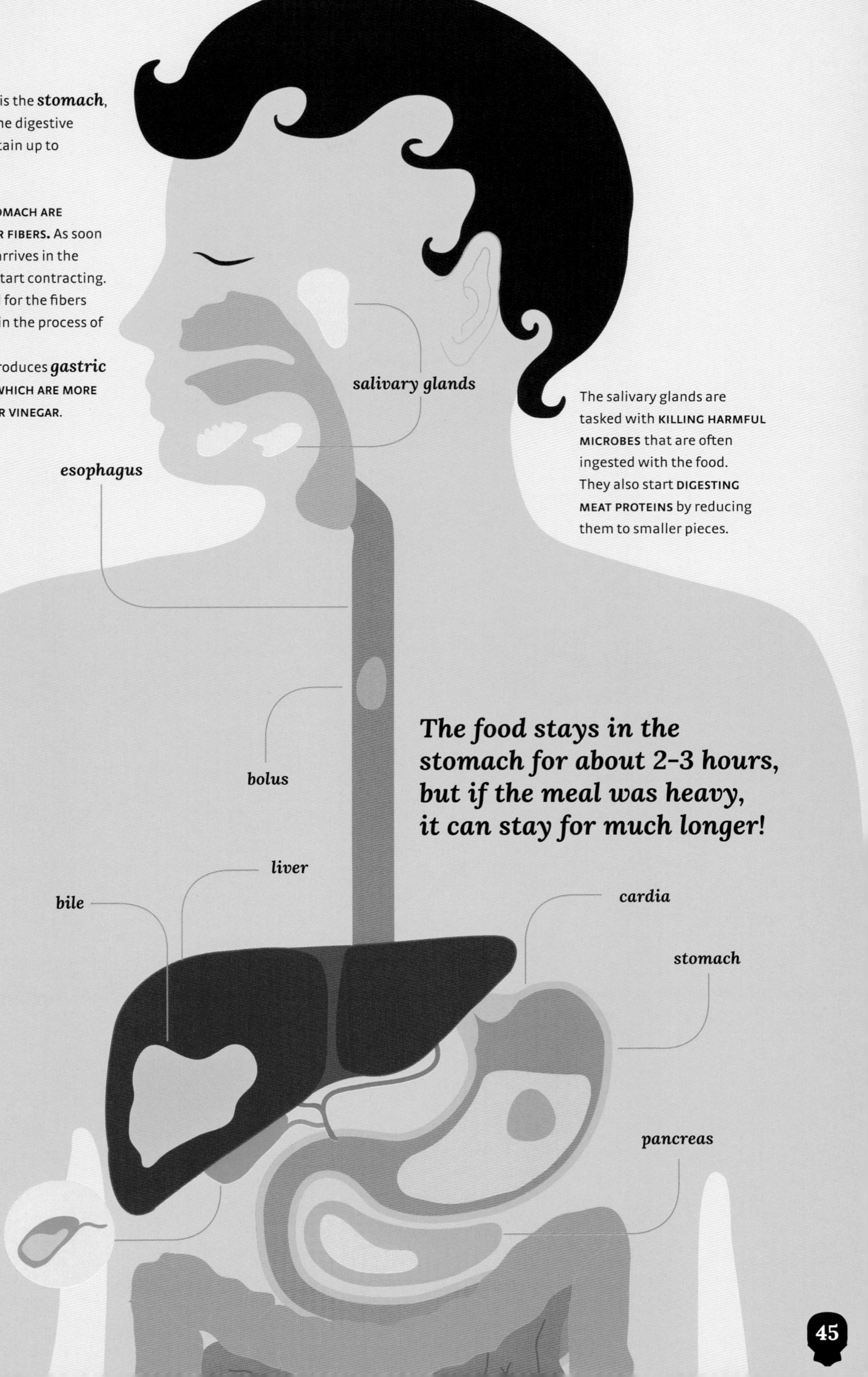

salivary glands

The salivary glands are tasked with KILLING HARMFUL MICROBES that are often ingested with the food. They also start DIGESTING MEAT PROTEINS by reducing them to smaller pieces.

esophagus

bolus

The food stays in the stomach for about 2–3 hours, but if the meal was heavy, it can stay for much longer!

liver

cardia

bile

stomach

pancreas

gallbladder

The helpers of the gastrointestinal tract

The liver

The gastrointestinal tract is helped in its work by two organs that make key contributions.

The first one is the *liver*, a big organ weighing approximately 4.5 lb (2 kg), which makes up almost 2.5% of the body weight.
The functions of the liver are many, but the one that aids *digestion* is the production of the *bile*, a dark yellow, viscous fluid. THE LIVER PRODUCES ABOUT 2 PT (1 L) OF BILE A DAY.

WHAT IS THE PURPOSE OF THE BILE?
It HELPS DIGEST THE FATS that come out of the stomach and go into the intestine.

The gallbladder

Part of the bile is stored, as a reserve, in a small **sac** connected to the liver, the *gallbladder*.

The pancreas

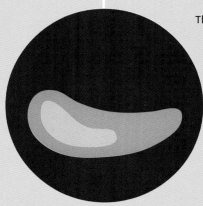

The second helper of the digestive tract is the *pancreas*, a small, slender organ of a salmon-pink color measuring 5-6 in (12-15 cm).
The pancreas carries out other important tasks for the body, but its main function in the digestive process is to produce the *pancreatic juice*.

This juice is a colorless liquid, 99% of which is made up of water. The pancreas produces between 1 and 4 pt (0.5-2 l) a day. Like the bile, this liquid is secreted into the first part of the intestine, and it is CRUCIAL BECAUSE IT HELPS DIGEST FATS AND PROTEINS.

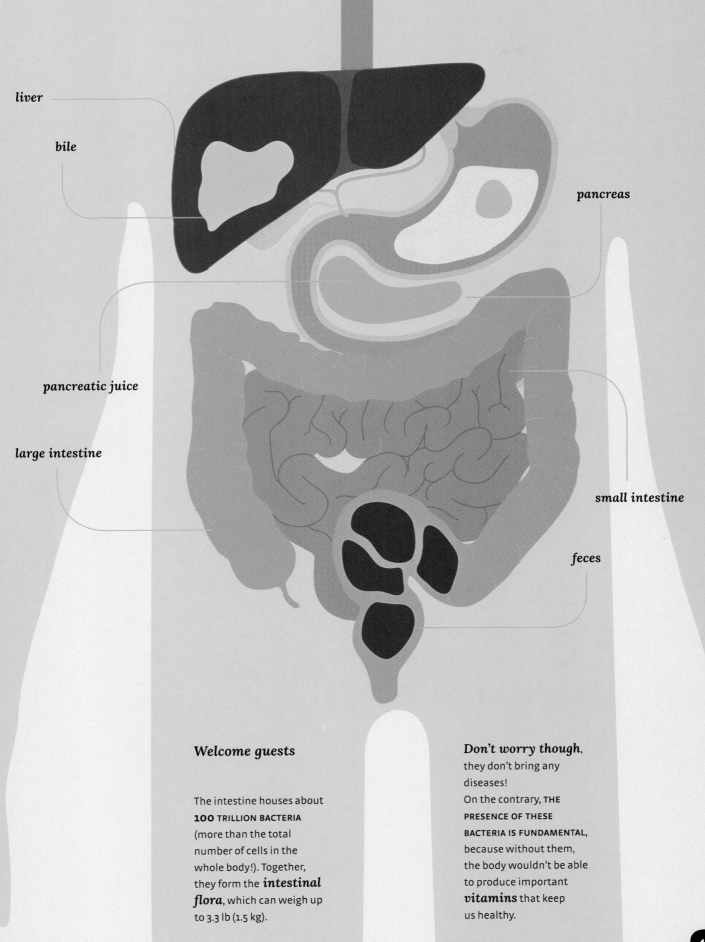

liver

bile

pancreas

pancreatic juice

large intestine

small intestine

feces

Welcome guests

The intestine houses about **100** TRILLION BACTERIA (more than the total number of cells in the whole body!). Together, they form the **intestinal flora**, which can weigh up to 3.3 lb (1.5 kg).

Don't worry though, they don't bring any diseases! On the contrary, THE PRESENCE OF THESE BACTERIA IS FUNDAMENTAL, because without them, the body wouldn't be able to produce important **vitamins** that keep us healthy.

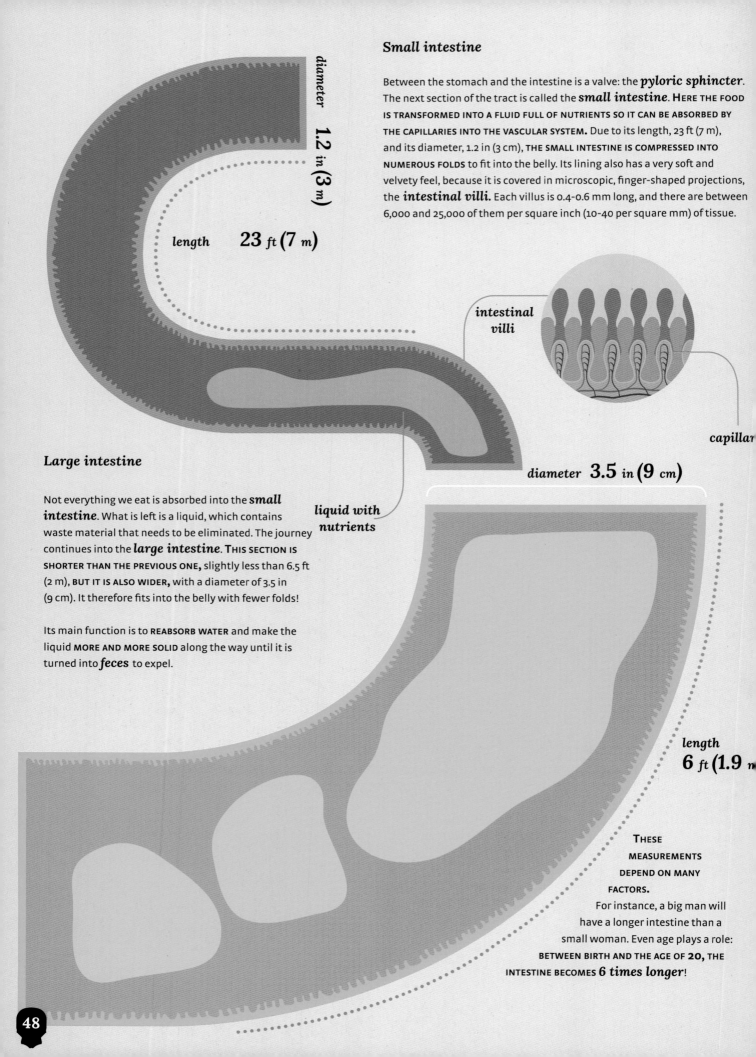

Small intestine

Between the stomach and the intestine is a valve: the **pyloric sphincter**. The next section of the tract is called the **small intestine**. HERE THE FOOD IS TRANSFORMED INTO A FLUID FULL OF NUTRIENTS SO IT CAN BE ABSORBED BY THE CAPILLARIES INTO THE VASCULAR SYSTEM. Due to its length, 23 ft (7 m), and its diameter, 1.2 in (3 cm), THE SMALL INTESTINE IS COMPRESSED INTO NUMEROUS FOLDS to fit into the belly. Its lining also has a very soft and velvety feel, because it is covered in microscopic, finger-shaped projections, the **intestinal villi**. Each villus is 0.4-0.6 mm long, and there are between 6,000 and 25,000 of them per square inch (10-40 per square mm) of tissue.

diameter **1.2** in **(3 m)**

length **23** ft **(7 m)**

intestinal villi

capillar

liquid with nutrients

diameter **3.5** in **(9 cm)**

Large intestine

Not everything we eat is absorbed into the **small intestine**. What is left is a liquid, which contains waste material that needs to be eliminated. The journey continues into the **large intestine**. THIS SECTION IS SHORTER THAN THE PREVIOUS ONE, slightly less than 6.5 ft (2 m), BUT IT IS ALSO WIDER, with a diameter of 3.5 in (9 cm). It therefore fits into the belly with fewer folds!

Its main function is to REABSORB WATER and make the liquid MORE AND MORE SOLID along the way until it is turned into **feces** to expel.

length **6** ft **(1.9 m)**

THESE MEASUREMENTS DEPEND ON MANY FACTORS.
For instance, a big man will have a longer intestine than a small woman. Even age plays a role: BETWEEN BIRTH AND THE AGE OF 20, THE INTESTINE BECOMES **6 times longer**!

What about animals?

Stomach

SOME MAMMALS DON'T HAVE JUST ONE STOMACH: THEY HAVE 4! They are called *grazers*. Examples include cows, deer, and antelope. These animals eat only plants. The plants must be eaten in HUGE QUANTITIES because they are not very rich in nutrients.

For the first part of the digestion process, they need MORE SPACE (meaning more stomachs) and MORE TIME. THE FOOD ACTUALLY COMES BACK INTO THE MOUTH TO BE CHEWED AGAIN (the *grazing*).

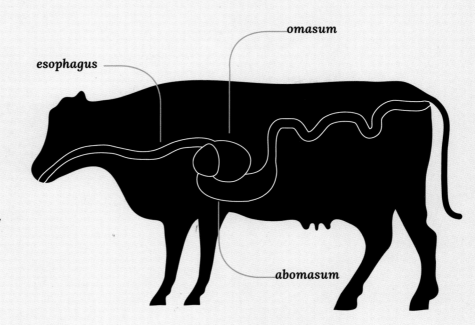

esophagus

omasum

abomasum

15 ft **(4.5 m)**

26-29 ft **(8-9 m)**

98 ft **(30 m)**

Intestine

The length of the intestine depends on the diet. We know that THE INTESTINE OF A HUMAN, WHICH IS AN OMNIVORE MAMMAL, IS 26-29 ft (8-9 m) LONG.

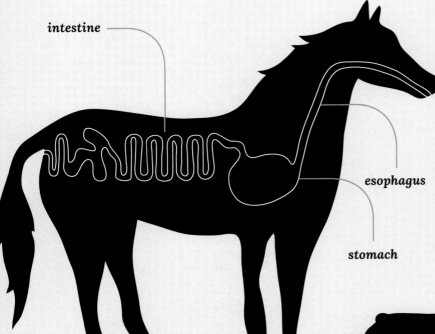

intestine

esophagus

stomach

The intestine of a carnivore, like a *leopard*, is much **shorter** – about 15 ft (4.5 m) – because meat is much more nutrient than vegetables and needs less of a journey to be digested. On the other hand, the intestine of a *horse*, which is a herbivore, measures up to **98 ft (30 m)**!

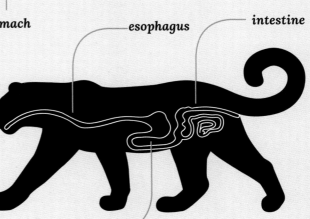

esophagus

intestine

stomach

49

Chewing and swallowing

Try and imagine eating an apple or a slice of pizza without being able to chew it... **IT WOULD BE IMPOSSIBLE!** Luckily, we have the **teeth** to chew our food.

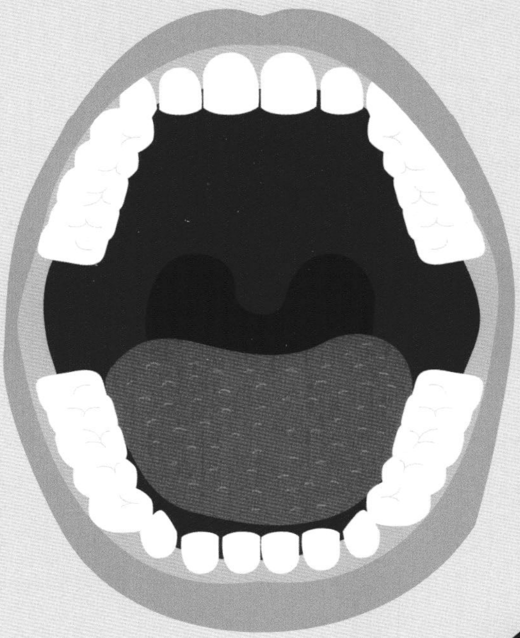

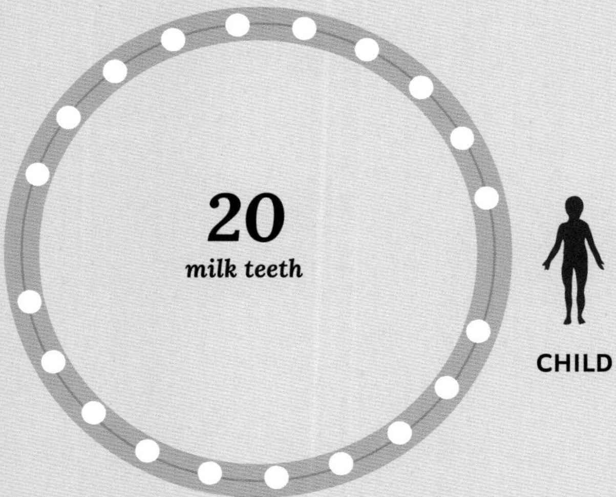

20
milk teeth

CHILD

ADULT

At birth, we have no teeth. We don't need them, because newborns only need milk. After about **6 MONTHS,** the teeth start coming out of the **gums**, and by the age of **6,** there are 20 of them. These are the **milk teeth**.

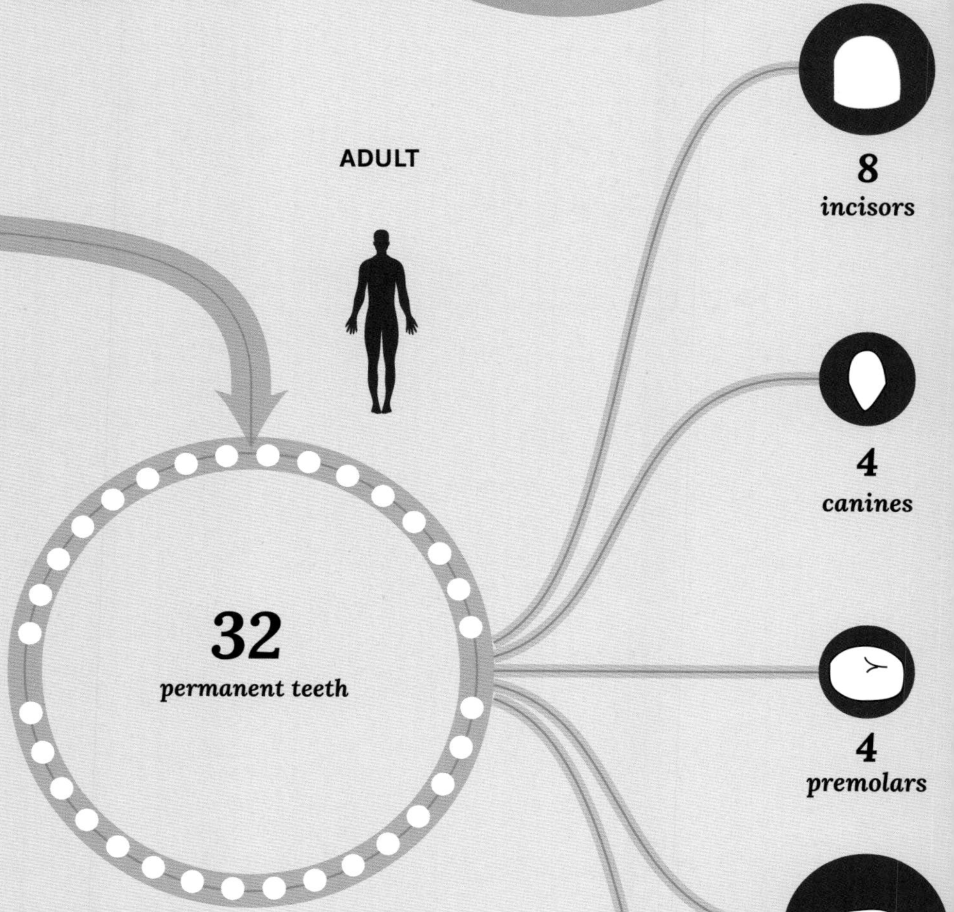

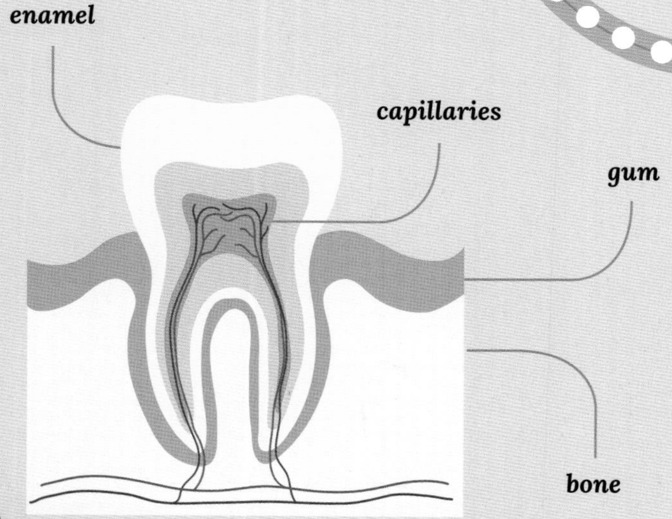

32
permanent teeth

enamel

capillaries

gum

When growing up, milk teeth are progressively replaced. Moreover, additonal teeth grow. **THE DENTITION (OR ARRANGEMENT) OF AN ADULT MOUTH IS MADE UP OF 32 teeth.**

bone

8
incisors

4
canines

4
premolars

12
molars

4
third molars

Guess who...

Adult humans have **32 teeth**, but not all mammals have dentitions like ours. Some species have no teeth at all, like the anteater or the whale. Others have over 40 teeth, like the bat or the mole.
The **different shapes of the teeth** are linked to specific functions, a bit like **tools**.

IN THE DRAWINGS BELOW, THE TEETH HAVE A NUMBER AND THE TOOLS HAVE AN ALPHABETIC LETTER. PAIR THE TYPE OF TOOTH WITH THE CORRECT TOOL. YOU'LL FIND THE SOLUTIONS AT THE BOTTOM OF THE PAGE.

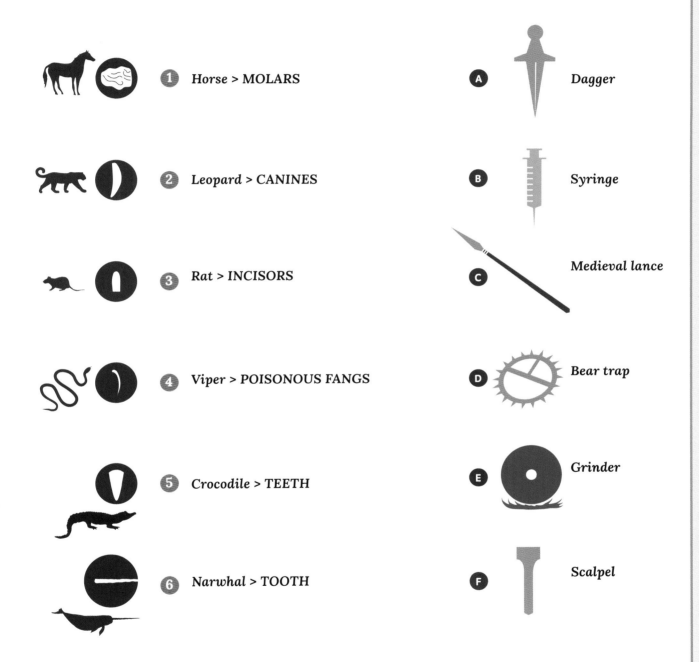

1 Horse > MOLARS

2 Leopard > CANINES

3 Rat > INCISORS

4 Viper > POISONOUS FANGS

5 Crocodile > TEETH

6 Narwhal > TOOTH

A Dagger

B Syringe

C Medieval lance

D Bear trap

E Grinder

F Scalpel

C 6   D 5   B 4   F 3   A 2   E 1

Sight

Capture the light

The world is full of light. During the day, we use the natural light that the sun sends us through its rays. At night, in the dark, we use artificial light created by electricity.

The eye

The light is captured by two "windows" opened on the world. We are talking about the **eyes**, the organs that are responsible for the sense of **sight**. But be aware that the eyes are only a device. Just like **cameras**, they record what we see. THE TRUE DIRECTOR IS THE BRAIN, which receives the images from the eyes and sees the **shapes**, the **colors**, and the **movements** of what we are watching.

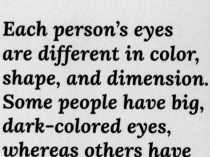

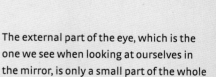

Each person's eyes are different in color, shape, and dimension. Some people have big, dark-colored eyes, whereas others have very small, light-colored eyes.

The external part of the eye, which is the one we see when looking at ourselves in the mirror, is only a small part of the whole **eyeball**.

Exactly like the Earth, THE EYE HAS THE SHAPE OF A SPHERE. It's as big as a ping pong ball and weighs almost **1 oz (30 g)**. From the rear part of the eyeball, a thick cord extends to reach the brain. This is called the **optic nerve**.

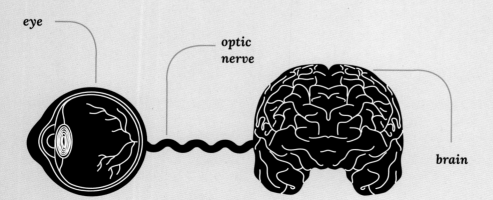

eye

optic nerve

brain

What is the anatomy of the eye?

In order to let the **light** in, the eye features a series of transparent elements, exactly like the lens equipment of a camera.
STARTING FROM THE OUTSIDE: The first transparent layer that the light goes through is the **cornea**, behind which is the first lens, a fluid called the **aqueous humor**. The cornea and the aqueous humor protect the **iris**, which is the colored part of the eye. The white part of the eye is called the **sclera**. We can see only a small section of it, but the sclera actually surrounds the whole eyeball.

At the center of the iris is a hole, the **pupil**, which contracts and shrinks depending on the amount of light that hits it. **WHEN THE LIGHT IS WEAK, THE PUPIL CAN DILATE UP TO 4 TIMES THE SIZE IT NORMALLY TAKES WHEN IT IS HIT BY INTENSE LIGHT.**

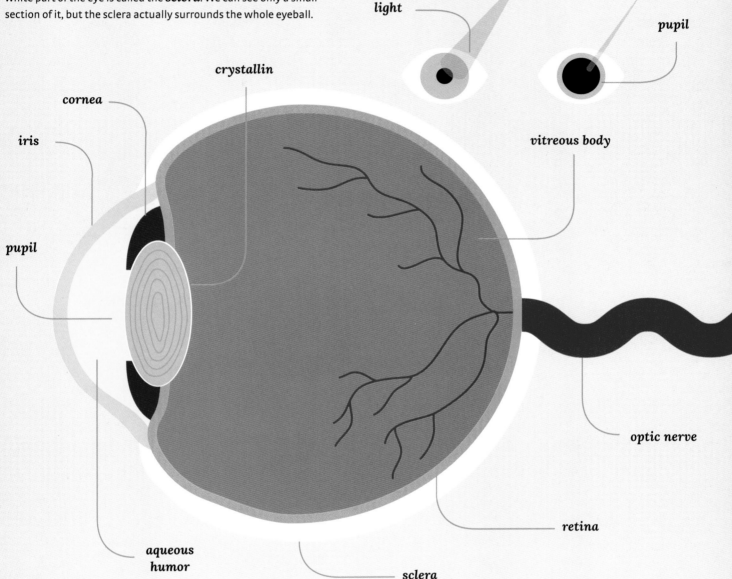

crystallin

cornea

iris

pupil

light

pupil

vitreous body

optic nerve

retina

aqueous humor

sclera

BEHIND THE IRIS IS THE SECOND LENS, the **crystallin**, which is more elastic and can change its shape to **ZOOM AND FOCUS IN** on what we are seeing. After the crystallin is **THE THIRD LENS**, the **vitreous body**, a clear, jelly-like substance that occupies most of the inside of the eyeball. All these steps are necessary to reach the part of the eye that is the most sensitive to light, i.e. the part that records the image: the **retina**. The retina is a membrane about **120 microns** thick (1 million microns make up 1 meter). It lines the entire internal part of the eyeball.

It is formed by many layers of cells that transform light stimuli into **nerve impulses** to send to the brain through the optic nerve.

Its cells have two types. Because of their shapes, the two types are called: **rods and cones.**
While **THE CONES ALLOW US TO SEE COLORS, THE RODS HELP US SEE WHEN THE LIGHT IS POOR.** The retina contains 6 million cones and 100 million rods!

Always moving

THE EYES NEVER STAY STILL. Thanks to 6 different muscles, they are able to move 3-5 *times per second*, constantly moving the focus on the object we are watching from one side to the other. The overall image is therefore never created by one glance, but by a multitude of brief glances at each part of the object. **THESE MOVEMENTS ARE VERY SIMILAR TO THOSE MADE BY THE ANTENNAE OF AN INSECT OR BY A MOUSE'S WHISKERS.** The purpose of antennae is to scan the surrounding environment, which is exactly what eyes do.

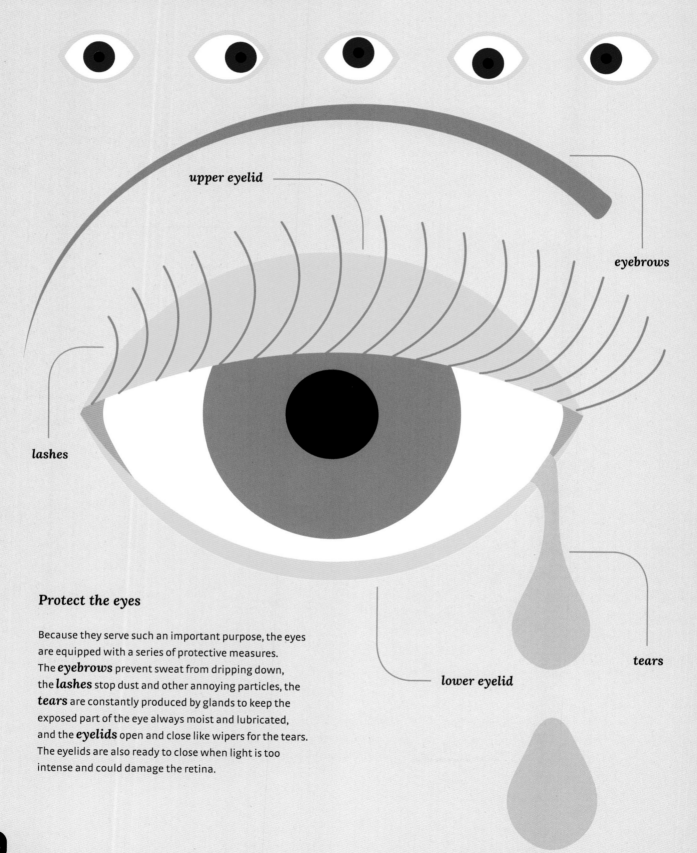

upper eyelid

eyebrows

lashes

tears

lower eyelid

Protect the eyes

Because they serve such an important purpose, the eyes are equipped with a series of protective measures. The **eyebrows** prevent sweat from dripping down, the **lashes** stop dust and other annoying particles, the **tears** are constantly produced by glands to keep the exposed part of the eye always moist and lubricated, and the **eyelids** open and close like wipers for the tears. The eyelids are also ready to close when light is too intense and could damage the retina.

What about animals?

The biggest eye ever observed belongs to the **giant squid**. The **diameter** of its eye **is over 12 in (30 cm)**.
If your eye is as big as a ping pong ball, the eye of this animal **is bigger than a basketball!**

GIANT SQUID

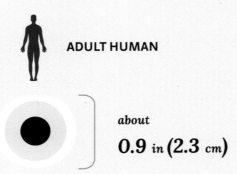

ADULT HUMAN

about
0.9 in (2.3 cm)

The big, protruding eyes of a CHAMELEON have a unique characteristic in the animal world: EACH EYE CAN ROTATE INDEPENDENTLY.

So while one eye can look downwards, the other can look upwards or sideways!

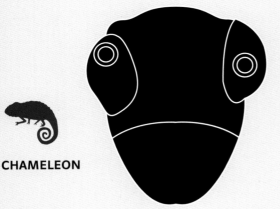

CHAMELEON

about
12 in (30 cm)

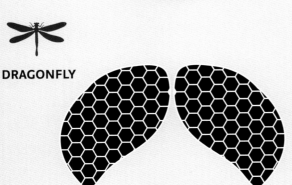

DRAGONFLY

THE EYES OF INSECTS ARE VERY SPECIAL. They are called COMPOUND EYES because they are made up of many tiny eyes called **ommatidias**, which are packed against one another. The eye of a **dragonfly** can comprise of over **30,000 ommatidias**. The single images captured by each ommatidium are sent to the brain, which then composes them like a jigsaw puzzle to form one complete image.

Hearing
Capture the sound

Your favorite song, the bell of a bike, or your parents' voices: all of these sounds are recognized only when they reach the brain.

From waves to sound

Before reaching the brain, the sound is just a **WAVE THAT VIBRATES IN THE SPACE.** It enters the *ear,* and after a complicated route, it turns into **nerve impulses** that reach the **cerebral cortex** through the **auditory nerve.** The brain classifies the sounds into categories like pleasant, annoying, etc. The ear is able to capture sounds even when we sleep. It can't be "turned off." We don't hear these sounds because the brain ignores them during sleep.

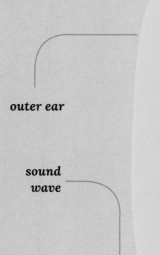

outer ear

sound wave

The ear, a stranger

What we call the "ear" is only *the outer ear*, the visible part of the organ responsible for hearing. It can have different appearances - big, small, sticking out, etc. - but its function is always that of **INTERCEPTING SOUND WAVES, EXACTLY LIKE A PARABOLIC ANTENNA.** In truth, the ear is a very complex structure and its most important parts are not visible. **LET'S DISCOVER THEM!**

ear canal

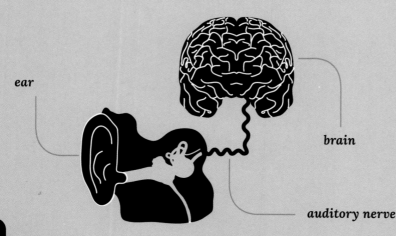

ear

brain

auditory nerve

Outer ear

Approximately halfway into the center of the outer ear is the hole of the ear canal, which is about **1 in (2.5 cm)** long and slightly over 0.2 in (0.5 cm) wide. The sound wave enters the canal and hits the **ear drum** - a membrane with a **diameter of about 0.4 in (10 mm)** - which is located at the end of the canal and makes it vibrate.

Middle ear

Beyond the ear drum is a sequence of three tiny bones connected to one another. Their names fit them perfectly because they recall their shapes: *malleus*, *incus*, and *stapes*.

THE MALLEUS IS ATTACHED TO THE EAR DRUM. IT RECEIVES VIBRATIONS FROM THE EAR DRUM AND TRANSMITS THEM TO THE INCUS AND THE STAPES. THE STAPES IS CONNECTED TO THE INNER EAR. The middle ear also has an empty space that works as a **sounding box** and amplifies the vibrations. From this space, a canal called the **Eustachian tube** extends and connects to the throat.

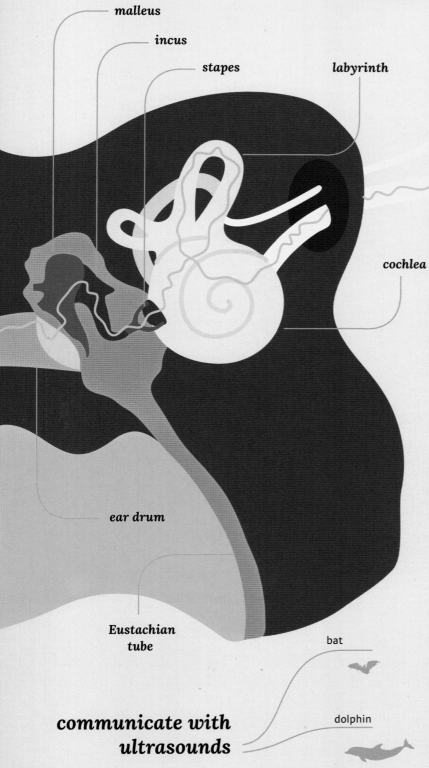

malleus

incus

stapes

labyrinth

auditory nerve

cochlea

ear drum

Eustachian tube

Inner ear

The structure of the inner ear is very complex. It is made up of a web of canals and passageways intricate enough to be called a **labyrinth**.
The whole labyrinth is filled up with a fluid which, under the stimulation of vibrations, moves and causes its huge quantity of tiny **hairs** to vibrate and send out **electric impulses**. One ear can have as many as 25,000 hairs! The labyrinth has a snail-shaped section from which the **auditory nerve** extends. The auditory nerve sends nerve impulses to the brain, where they are eventually transformed into **sounds**.

Ultrasounds and infrasounds

The sounds you hear are only part of the sound vibrations in the air. There are much higher sounds, called **ultrasounds**, and much lower ones, called **infrasounds**, which can be intercepted only by certain animals.

communicate with infrasounds

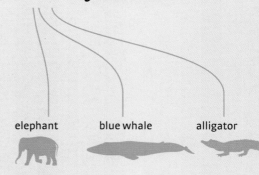

bat

dolphin

elephant

blue whale

alligator

communicate with ultrasounds

A **bat** is sensitive to ultrasounds and uses them to orient itself and to find its prey. When flying, it emits **very high-pitched vibrations** that come back to it like an echo after they meet an obstacle. A **dolphin** does the same thing: sound waves travel through water as well.

Whales, elephants, and alligators can produce and intercept infrasounds.
IN GENERAL, THE ANIMALS THAT ARE ABLE TO INTERCEPT INFRASOUNDS ARE THE LARGER ONES.

Smell and Taste

Fragrant and good

The five senses in our bodies work together so that we can get to know the world around us. Two of these senses are inseparable. They are located in the nose and mouth: smell and taste.

When we have a cold, we often can't taste the food we are eating. This is because the cold interferes with how our noses work. Smell has an important role in how we taste food.

Mmm, what a nice smell! Bleah, it stinks!

The air we breathe is always packed with all sorts of scents. **THE HUMAN BEING IS AMONG THOSE ANIMALS LEAST SENSITIVE TO SCENTS** (think about the incredible sense of smell of a hunting dog, for example). However, it is estimated that we can **RECOGNIZE UP TO 10,000 DIFFERENT SCENTS**. This is only true when the particles creating the scent are very concentrated in the air. In order to smell a scent better, we need to sniff, meaning we need to use our noses to draw in the air near the object of interest.

brain

olfactory nerve

nose

The inner part of the nose is lined with almost **20 million olfactory cells** (a dog's nose has up to 200 million!). Each cell features a microscopic **hair** that transforms the scent into nerve impulses to send to the brain through the olfactory nerve.
Hearing is the sense that best protects us against potential dangers. But before seeing or hearing a fire, the smell of smoke can alert us, the same way disgusting smells from food can tell us if it is rotten.

olfactory cells

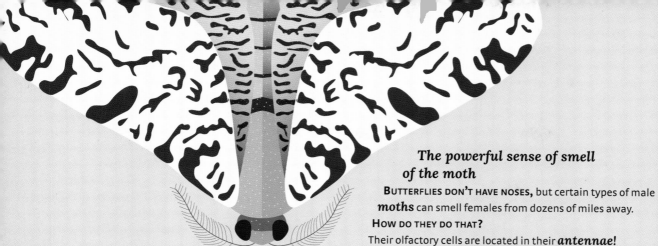

The powerful sense of smell of the moth

BUTTERFLIES DON'T HAVE NOSES, but certain types of male **moths** can smell females from dozens of miles away.
HOW DO THEY DO THAT?
Their olfactory cells are located in their **antennae!**

A tentacular nose

All species of **mole** have a very enhanced sense of smell, but there is one species that beats them all:
ITS NOSE FEATURES 22 TENTACLES. Each tentacle has about **100,000 cells** that capture scents and help the animal find worms and **insects** underground.

Stay away!

There are animals with defense mechanisms based on the sense of smell. The most famous is the **skunk**, which is equipped with **glands** that produce a very unpleasant and piercing smell. By spraying the bad smell into the air, this animal tries to scare or ward off potential enemies. They can also use the spray to stun prey.

Scented flowers

It's romantic to think that **flowers** have nice scents just to make our gardens more enjoyable … but the truth is that they need these scents to **reproduce**. Bats, insects, and birds like the **hummingbird** have very sensitive senses of smell. The scent of flowers attracts them. While feeding on the **nectar** of the flowers, the animals become covered in pollen and unknowingly TRANSFER IT FROM FLOWER TO FLOWER, ALLOWING FERTILIZATION TO HAPPEN!

Look at your tongue in the mirror. You should see a lot of small bumps! These are called **papillae**. On the surface of the papillae are the **taste buds**. The taste buds are groups of cells connected to very thin nerves that CARRY IMPULSES TO THE BRAIN and recognize different flavors.

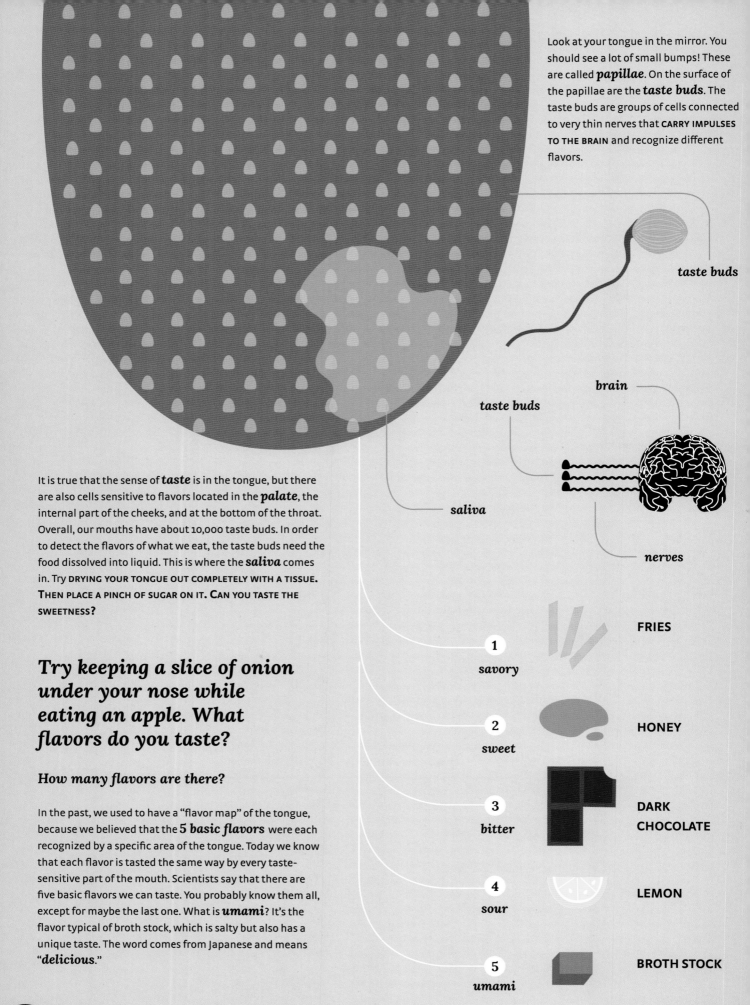

taste buds

taste buds

brain

saliva

nerves

It is true that the sense of **taste** is in the tongue, but there are also cells sensitive to flavors located in the **palate**, the internal part of the cheeks, and at the bottom of the throat. Overall, our mouths have about 10,000 taste buds. In order to detect the flavors of what we eat, the taste buds need the food dissolved into liquid. This is where the **saliva** comes in. Try DRYING YOUR TONGUE OUT COMPLETELY WITH A TISSUE. THEN PLACE A PINCH OF SUGAR ON IT. CAN YOU TASTE THE SWEETNESS?

Try keeping a slice of onion under your nose while eating an apple. What flavors do you taste?

How many flavors are there?

In the past, we used to have a "flavor map" of the tongue, because we believed that the **5 basic flavors** were each recognized by a specific area of the tongue. Today we know that each flavor is tasted the same way by every taste-sensitive part of the mouth. Scientists say that there are five basic flavors we can taste. You probably know them all, except for maybe the last one. What is **umami**? It's the flavor typical of broth stock, which is salty but also has a unique taste. The word comes from Japanese and means "**delicious**."

1 savory — FRIES

2 sweet — HONEY

3 bitter — DARK CHOCOLATE

4 sour — LEMON

5 umami — BROTH STOCK

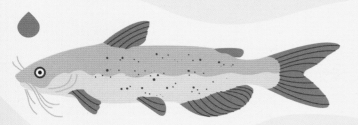

Taste with the tail

The **catfish** is the animal with THE HIGHEST NUMBER OF TASTE BUDS IN THE WORLD. It has them not only on the tongue, but also on the lips, head, and all over its body, including on its tail.

In particular, the channel catfish (*Ictalurus punctatus*) is the vertebrate with the most-sophisticated sense of taste . IT CAN CAPTURE THE TASTE OF A SINGLE DROP OF A CERTAIN SUBSTANCE DILUTED IN THE WATER OF AN OLYMPIC SWIMMING POOL!

Monarch and viceroy

The **monarch butterfly** is venomous and tastes really bad to predators. This is exactly what protects it. Monarchs also have very bright, unique colors. When a bird tastes one, it learns about the bad taste. In the future, its sense of taste will remind it not to eat butterflies with those colors!

monarch butterfly

However, the **viceroy butterfly** is even more clever. Its colors are almost the same as the bad-tasting monarch. Even though it is edible, most predators don't bother going near it!

viceroy butterfly

The salt of life

EVERY ANIMAL NEEDS A CERTAIN AMOUNT OF SALT IN ITS DIET. The ones that only eat vegetables need to get their salt elsewhere. The fine sense of taste of **Amazon parrots,** for example, allows them to easily find something salty to add to their diets. The birds gather in large numbers on salt-rich clay walls and eat small fragments.

Reproduction

Parents and children

Every living creature has the ability to reproduce. Individual creatures die sooner or later, but their species carries on through their offspring, who will also produce new individuals. The wonderful mechanism of reproduction has been going on since life first appeared on Earth billions of years ago.

Different organisms, different ways

The types of reproduction vary greatly, from the simplest one in **unicellular organisms** to the most complex one in **mammals**.

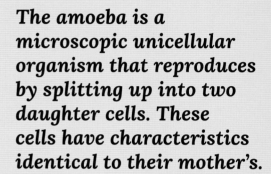

The amoeba is a microscopic unicellular organism that reproduces by splitting up into two daughter cells. These cells have characteristics identical to their mother's.

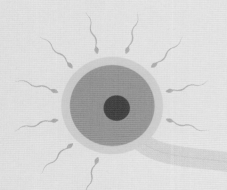

fertilization

Most animals instead need two parents in order to reproduce. Each parent produces a specific type of cell, called a **gamete.** Male gametes are the **spermatozoa**, and female gametes are the **eggs**.

zygote

New lives

In order for new life to occur, there needs to be **fertilization**, during which the TWO GAMETES, MALE AND FEMALE, FUSE TOGETHER TO BECOME ONE CELL. Crowds of spermatozoa compete with one another to reach the egg first, but **only one will become the winner,** i.e. only one will manage to penetrate the egg and fertilize it. The fertilized cell, called a **zygote**, divides into 2 cells, then 4, then 8, and so on. The speed at which these initial multiplications happen varies from animal to animal.

After several multiplications and transformations, the zygote becomes a small **embryo** that will nestle cozily in the lining of the **uterus**. FOR 9 MONTHS, THE EMBRYO WILL DEVELOP HERE UNTIL THE MOMENT OF BIRTH.

Free accommodation

FOR A DEVELOPING BABY, THE UTERUS IS A VERY SAFE AND COMFORTABLE SPACE.
In order to grow, the baby needs **nourishment,** and nature has come up with an ingenious system to meet this need. THE CIRCULATORY SYSTEM OF THE MOTHER IS CONNECTED TO THE BABY through a small tube, which is 19-24 in (50-60 cm) long and about 0.8 in (2 cm) thick. This tube is called the **umbilical cord**. Whatever the mother eats, the baby eats too. The tube is also how THE BABY'S BLOOD BECOMES OXYGENATED.

A natural swimming pool

During the entire pregnancy period, the fetus is immersed in a fluid, called **amniotic fluid**, that protects the baby from impacts and muffles the noises from the external world. It also keeps the baby's environment comfortable.

lining of the uterus

umbilical cord

fetus

amniotic fluid

30 hours

2 cells

2 and a half days

4 cells

4 days

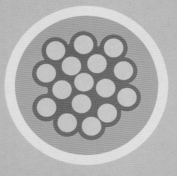

16 cells

Month after month

The pregnancy ends with the **labor**, when the baby is born. During its first months of life, the newborn is still dependent on its mother for food. Like all mammals, human mothers produce a very nutritious food: the **milk**.

2 Months
1.2 _in_ (3 _cm_)

3 Months
2.7 _in_ (7 _cm_)

5 Months
10 _in_ (25 _cm_)

The fetus moves and opens and closes its hands. It also **KICKS AND DOES SOMERSAULTS.** The mother's large belly is highly visible.

7 Months
16 _in_ (40 _cm_)

The fetus curls up in the uterus, with less and less room to move.

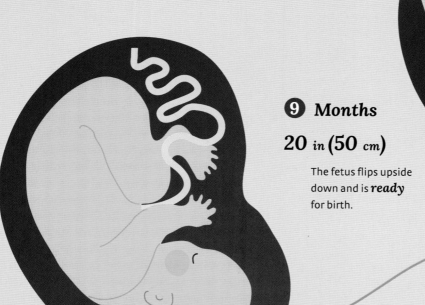

9 Months
20 _in_ (50 _cm_)

The fetus flips upside down and is **ready** for birth.

What about animals?

While fish, amphibians, reptiles, and birds, with a few rare exceptions, lay their **eggs**, all other mammals have a gestation period similar to humans, although it tends to be shorter.

ELEPHANT	22 months
GIRAFFE	15 months
WALRUS	15 months
HORSE	11 months
COW	9.5 months
HUMAN	9 months
GORILLA	8.5 months
CHIMPANZEE	8 months
HIPPO	8 months
LION	3.5 months
DOG	2 months
CAT	2 months
RABBIT	1 month
RAT	22 days

A comfortable skin pocket

Some mammals have very short pregnancies because their babies come out of the uterus way before reaching full development. One example is the **marsupial**. The tiny cubs spend the last part of their development inside a pouch, the famous pouch of the kangaroo, where they suck the milk they need to grow.

Egg-laying mammals

The **platypus** and the echidna are very strange animals. Although they are true **mammals** in every respect, **they lay eggs.**

Genetics

Same but different

Look around while you're walking down the street, riding a bus, or sitting in a classroom with your friends. Can you find anyone with a face identical to yours?

The answer is no. There might be a friend with the same height or the same eye color, but the facial features of your faces will never be perfectly identical. **You are unique.** No one like you has ever lived before, and they never will!

Each of the 8 billion inhabitants of the Earth is unique. But there is an exception: monozygotic twins.

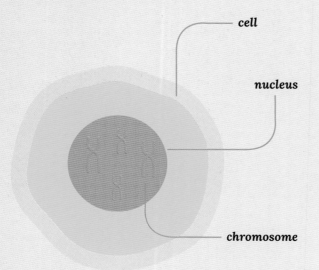

cell

nucleus

chromosome

You might look very similar to your brother or your sister, or to one of your parents. **WHERE DO THESE DIFFERENCES AND SIMILARITIES BETWEEN PEOPLE COME FROM?**
The branch of science that answers this question is called **genetics**.

DNA

Genetics studies the transfer of **characters** such as eye and hair color, skin color, or behavioral temperament. These characters ARE PASSED FROM PARENTS TO CHILDREN through generations. We call this **heredity**.

G like gene

The characteristics that we inherit are contained in the **genes**, which are small portions of a VERY COMPLEX MOLECULE (with a very complex name!), the **deoxyribonucleic acid**, better known as **DNA**.
The DNA is like an instruction manual. Inside, it has all the instructions on how the body has to be built and how it must work.

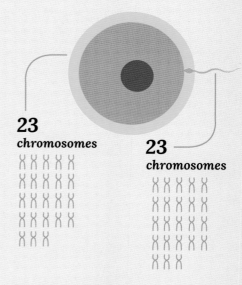

23 chromosomes

23 chromosomes

23 + 23 = 46

When a cell in the body is about to divide into two daughter cells, the chains of DNA inside the nucleus gather to form small, thread-like structures called **chromosomes**.
Each living species has a fixed number of chromosome pairs inside the nucleus of their cells. HUMANS HAVE 23 PAIRS, OR 46 CHROMOSOMES IN TOTAL. Only two types of cells are different: the **egg** and the **spermatozoon**. Each only has 23 chromosomes. The egg and the spermatozoon fuse together during fertilization.

This means that the **zygote**, the cell resulting from the union of the egg and the spermatozoon, will have **46 chromosomes**. The newborn will have a mix of characters from the father and the mother and will resemble them, but won't be identical.

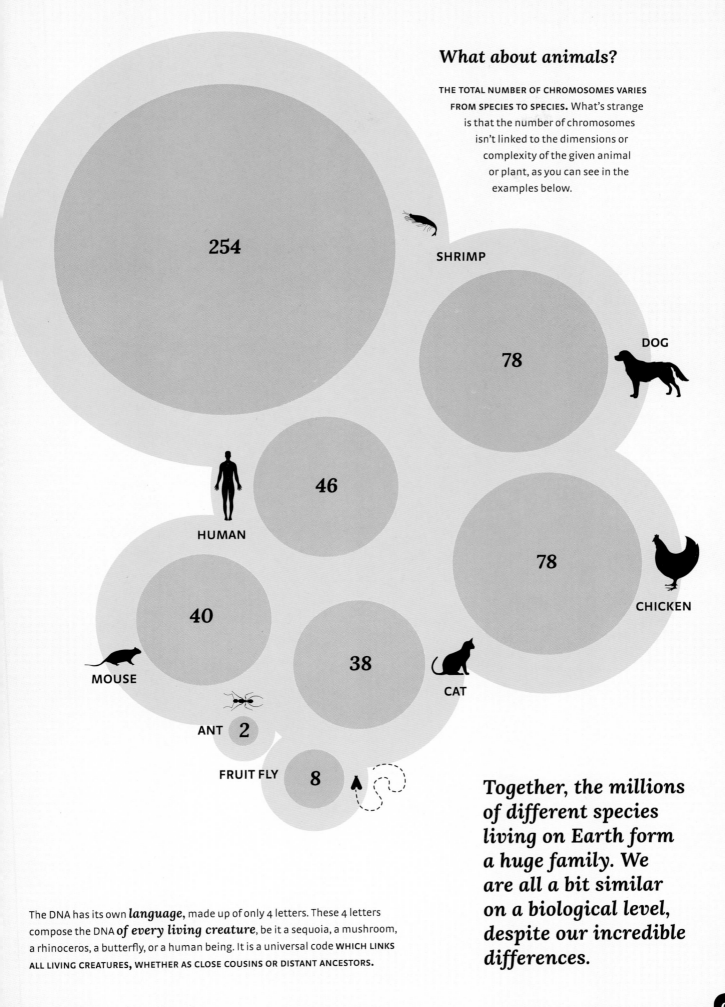

What about animals?

THE TOTAL NUMBER OF CHROMOSOMES VARIES FROM SPECIES TO SPECIES. What's strange is that the number of chromosomes isn't linked to the dimensions or complexity of the given animal or plant, as you can see in the examples below.

254

SHRIMP

78

DOG

46

HUMAN

78

CHICKEN

40

MOUSE

38

CAT

ANT **2**

FRUIT FLY **8**

Together, the millions of different species living on Earth form a huge family. We are all a bit similar on a biological level, despite our incredible differences.

The DNA has its own **language,** made up of only 4 letters. These 4 letters compose the DNA **of every living creature,** be it a sequoia, a mushroom, a rhinoceros, a butterfly, or a human being. It is a universal code **WHICH LINKS ALL LIVING CREATURES, WHETHER AS CLOSE COUSINS OR DISTANT ANCESTORS.**

Glossary

A

ALVEOLUS
Small air sac placed at the end of each bronchiole. It's through its walls that two gases are exchanged. With inhalation, oxygen is absorbed, and with exhalation, carbon dioxide is expelled.

AMNIOTIC FLUID
Fluid in which the baby is immersed during pregnancy. It protects the baby from impacts and helps keep its environment warm and comfortable.

ARTERY
Blood vessel with thick and elastic walls. The aorta artery extends from the left ventricle of the heart and branches out through the whole body to carry oxygenated blood. The pulmonary artery extends from the right ventricle and brings the oxygen-poor blood to the lungs.

ATRIUM
One of the chambers of the heart. There is a left and a right one. The right one is filled with the oxygen-poor blood brought in by the veins; in the left one, the pulmonary vein brings in the oxygenated blood coming from the lungs.

AXON
Long, slender projection of the nerve cell (or neuron). It transmits nerve impulses to the neurons or to the muscular fibers.

B

BILE
A dark yellow fluid produced by the liver that pours into the intestine to help food digestion.

C

CAPILLARY
A blood vessel as thin as a hair that is able to reach all cells in the body to bring them the nutrients and the oxygen necessary for survival.

CARBON DIOXIDE
Waste gas produced by the cells that is absorbed by the capillaries throughout the body and carried to the lungs, where it will be expelled through exhalation.

CARDIA
Valve placed between the esophagus and the stomach. It closes when the swallowed bolus ends up in the stomach, to prevent it from going back into the esophagus.

CELL
Fundamental component of the body of every organism. It is a microscopic living creature in itself, because it needs nutrients, it breathes, and it reproduces.

CEREBRAL CORTEX
Superficial layer of the brain that holds the cerebral circumvolutions, i.e. very deep folds that give it the typical "crumpled" look. It is in the cortex - which is particularly thick in the human being - that the abilities typical of human beings reside: thought, memory, attention, etc.

CHROMOSOME
A microscopic, thread-like structure made up of DNA filaments. It becomes visible in the nucleus when a cell is about to divide into two daughter cells. The number of chromosomes is fixed for each living species. Human beings have 23 pairs.

COCHLEA
A specific structure inside the inner ear, with the shape similar to a snail, from which the auditory nerve departs to reach the brain.

CONES
Cells specific to the retina that allow the eye to see colors.

CORNEA
The outermost clear layer of the eye. It is the first part of the eye to receive light from the environment, helping us to see.

DENDRITES

Thin extensions of the nerve cell (the neuron) that, all together, look like tree branches. Their purpose is to transmit nerve impulses to the neuron.

DERMIS

Layer of the skin under the epidermis. The dermis houses the touch receptors, the hair follicles, the sebaceous cysts, and the sweat glands.

DIAPHRAGM

Large, dome-shaped muscle that separates the chest from the abdomen. Its function is fundamental for breathing. When it contracts, air enters the lungs, and when it relaxes, air is expelled.

DNA

Acronym for deoxyribonucleic acid. It is a molecule situated inside the nucleus of each cell and is necessary for cellular reproduction.

EAR DRUM

Membrane situated at the end of the ear canal, separating the outer ear from the middle ear. When the ear drum is hit by a sound wave, it vibrates and consequently makes the following structures in the middle and inner ear vibrate too.

EMBRYO

First stage of the development of a new individual inside the maternal uterus. After the second month of pregnancy, we no longer call it an embryo, but a fetus.

EPIDERMIS

Outermost layer of skin. Its cells are continuously replaced as they die, and new cells take their place. The epidermis is one of the ways our body eliminate certain types of waste.

ERITHROCYTE

Blood cell better known as red blood cell. It is very small, has a bright red color, and is produced by the bone marrow. In our blood, there are normally 4-6 million erythrocytes per cubic millimeter.

EUSTACHIAN TUBE

Canal that connects the middle ear to the throat and serves as a sounding box.

EXHALATION

Phase of the breathing that expels carbon dioxide-rich air from the lungs.

FERTILIZATION

Initial stage of reproduction, during which the male gamete - the spermatozoon - penetrates the female gamete - the egg, thus beginning a new life.

FETUS

A new individual developing inside the uterus, from the second month of pregnancy up to labor.

FIBER (MUSCULAR)

Cell of the muscular system with an elongated shape. It has the ability to contract and stretch. There are striated cells, typical of voluntary muscles, and smooth cells, typical of involuntary muscles. The fibers in the cardiac muscle are the only ones that are striated and involuntary.

FLORA (INTESTINE)

Bacteria living inside our intestine, crucial for the production of certain vitamins. Overall, the intestinal flora can weigh up to 3.3 lb (1.5 kg).

FREQUENCY (CARDIAC)

Number of heartbeats per minute. It increases when under exertion.

FREQUENCY (RESPIRATORY)

Number of breaths per minute. It increases when under exertion.

GALLBLADDER

Small, pouch-like organ that serves as storage for the bile produced by the liver. The two are connected via a small canal. The gallbladder empties its contents in the intestine when needed.

GAMETE

Cell that is needed for reproduction. The female gamete is the egg, and the male gamete is the spermatozoon.

GENE

Small portion of DNA that contains the information of about certain hereditary characteristics.

HEMOGLOBIN

Protein contained in the red blood cells, but also found loose in small quantities in the blood. Its task is to accumulate oxygen that the blood then carries to each cell.

INFRASOUNDS

Sound waves with a very low vibration frequency that cannot be heard by the human ear.

INHALATION

Phase of the breathing, during which air enters the lungs.

IRIS

Membrane of the eye, of variable color, situated behind the cornea. The iris determines the color of our eyes. It can be black, brown, blue, or green. It has the shape of a ring, with a hole in the center, the pupil, which allows light to travel through the eye until it reaches the retina.

LABYRINTH

Part of the ear made up of a series of intricate canals filled with a fluid called endolymph. The vibrations of the sound waves reach the labyrinth and make the endolymph vibrate too, which then transmits a nerve impulse to the brain through the auditory nerve.

LEUCOCYTE

Blood cell better known as a white blood cell. There are 5 types, but they all have the function of protecting the body against attacks from foreign particles that often carry diseases.

MELANIN

Black pigment contained inside the cells that contributes to the darkness or lightness of our complexions and determines the color of the eyes and hair.

MICRON

One millionth of a meter.

NEURON

Cell of the nervous system that receives all external stimuli and gives orders to the other organs. Its shape is very peculiar (it looks like a tree), with the axon as a trunk and the dendrites as branches. Through the dendrites and the axon, each neuron connects to thousands of other nerve cells, creating a thick web that the nerve impulses run through.

PAPILLAE

Small protuberances of different shapes that are mainly found in the tongue, but also on the palate and on the inside of the cheeks. On their surfaces are the taste buds, which are nerve receptors sensitive to taste.

PLASMA

Liquid part of the blood, making up for 55% of its total volume. The remaining 45% is made up of cells, erythrocytes, leucocytes, and platelets

PLATELET

Blood cell of tiny dimensions and with an irregular shape. Platelets are crucial in the process of the coagulation of the blood.

PREGNANCY

Period during which the baby develops inside the uterus. In the human species, pregnancy lasts 9 months.

PUPIL

Round hole at the center of the iris that allows the light to proceed through the eye and reach the retina. Its dimensions vary depending on the intensity of light. It becomes smaller when the light is strong and larger when the light is weak.

PYLORUS

Valve between the stomach and the first part of the small intestine. It closes after the bolus of food reaches the intestine, preventing it from returning to the stomach.

RECEPTOR

Nerve structure that receives a stimulus and transforms it into a nerve impulse. For example, a light stimulus is caught by a photoreceptor.

RETINA

Membrane sensitive to light that lines the internal wall of the eyeball. It is a very delicate structure made up of very specialized cells, the cones and the rods, which transform the light stimuli into nerve impulses to send to the brain through the optic nerve.

RODS

Cells specific to the retina that allow our eyes to see even in the shade, which is when the light is very weak.

TISSUE

A group of similar cells that carry out the same functions. In the human body, tissues fall into 4 types: epithelial, muscular, nervous, and connective.

ULTRASOUNDS

Sound waves with a very high-pitched frequency that cannot be heard by the human ear.

VEIN

Blood vessel with inflexible walls. It is equipped with valves, which force the blood to flow only in one direction. The two venae cavae, superior and inferior, take the oxygen-poor blood to the right atrium, while the pulmonary vein brings the oxygenated blood from the lungs into the left atrium.

VENTRICLE

One of the chambers of the heart. There is a right and a left one. From the left ventricle, the aorta departs, branching out through the whole body and carrying oxygenated blood. From the right ventricle, the pulmonary artery sends the oxygen-poor blood to the lungs, where it will be made full of oxygen again.

VILLI (INTESTINE)

Microscopic, finger-shaped protuberances that line the internal walls of the small intestine. Their function is to increase the surface through which the nutrients are absorbed into the blood stream.

ZYGOTE

Cell resulting from the fusion of two gametes, the egg and the spermatozoon. It is the first cell of a new life.

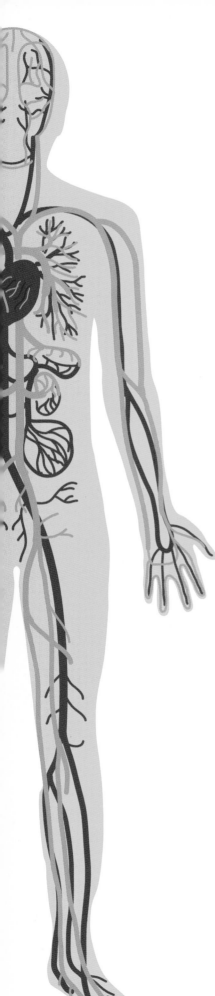

Cristina Peraboni

A veterinarian with a passion for natural science, she has always worked in scientific publishing and edutainment and organizes training courses for teachers and museum educators.
She collaborates with several publishing houses, curating publications for children and adults. In the past years she has realized several books for White Star Kids.

Giulia De Amicis

After completing a master's degree in communication design in 2012, Giulia began working as a visual designer and illustrator. Her work primarily consists of presenting information visually for newspapers, magazines, and associations in the environmental sector, with a particular focus on marine ecology, geography, and human rights.
She has recently illustrated several publications for White Star Kids.

Graphic layout
Valentina Figus

White Star Kids® is a registered trademark property of White Star s.r.l.

© 2019 White Star s.r.l.
Piazzale Luigi Cadorna, 6
20123 Milan, Italy
www.whitestar.it

Revised Edition

Translation: Inga Sempel

ISBN 978-88-544-1528-7
1 2 3 4 5 6   23 22 21 20 19

Printed in China

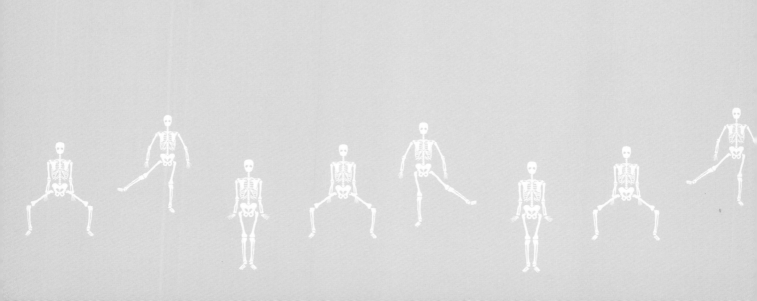